I0456932

While Waiting *for* Morning

an invitation to pray

DENISE J. HUGHES

TABLE OF CONTENTS

Part One: People of Prayer

Part Two: Principles of Prayer

Part Three: Practices of Prayer

People

of

Prayer

CHAPTER 1

Praying in the Dark

"I pray to God—my life a prayer—and wait for what he'll say and do. My life's on the line before God, my Lord, waiting and watching till morning, waiting and watching till morning."

Psalm 130:5-6 (MSG)

I woke up.

I didn't know where I was or how I got there or even what day of the week it was, but as I looked around the room, it was clear I was in a hospital bed. I had an IV in each arm, and I was wearing a hospital gown, except I didn't know who put it on me or who took off the clothes I had been wearing.

The table next to me had a framed picture of my family and our two golden pups. I smiled in relief. If that was there, my people must know where I am. Then, across the room on a white dry erase board, I saw my husband's handwriting: *I'll be back at 4 AM. I love you. ~ Jeff.* The black-rimmed clock on the wall said two o'clock, but the room didn't have a window to see outside. I couldn't tell if it was 2:00 in the morning or the afternoon.

A nurse walked in and asked me, "How are you feeling?"

"I feel fine. Except. Where am I?"

The nurse told me the name of the hospital.

"Okay, I don't live too far from here, and this is my family." I pointed to the picture on the table.

"Yes, I met them earlier." The nurse moved closer to check my vitals.

"Um, that message on the board is from my husband. He's going to be here at 4 AM, and it's two o'clock now, but I can't tell if it's AM or PM."

"It's the middle of the night," the nurse responded.

This was good news. It meant Jeff would arrive in a couple of hours. Then I asked, "Why am I here?"

With a quiet somberness the nurse said, "You have a blood clot in your brain."

I absorbed this news with dread. This was bad. Really bad. I'd been hospitalized four years earlier for blood clots in my lungs. It had taken months to recover, and I had prayed specifically that God wouldn't allow any more blood clots to form in my body ever again. But now I have one in my brain?

In response to this news, I had one thought: *God, you didn't answer my prayer.*

Despite this terrible news, I remained surprisingly calm—probably because of all the drugs they had me on— and I started asking a lot of medical questions. I learned I'd been in a coma for three days, hooked up to a ventilator, a feeding tube, and a PICC line. The previous day I had opened my eyes briefly and started breathing on my own again, so they had taken me off the breathing machine. But I continued to drift in and out of sleep.

The nurse offered me something to drink, so I gladly gulped down a tiny box of apple juice, noticing my throat hurt from being intubated. Then I settled in for the rest of the night, wide awake and waiting for my husband to come. With nothing to do but stare at the clock, I talked to God while waiting for morning. Not out loud, of course, but inside my mind. I had a lot to say.

What am I facing here, God? How long will I be in the hospital this time? What will the recovery process look like? Why didn't you answer my prayer? Why is this happening?

God invites us to come to him with our cares and concerns, so I've never been one to hold back. The psalms especially model for us the way of lament. My background is teaching language, literature, and composition, so I've studied the poetry and passion of the psalms for years. Nearly 40% of the psalms are songs of lament; they're desperate cries for help.[1] But in every psalm of lament there's always a point of turning. The tone will shift from despair to hope. It might be subtle, but it's there. Except in one.

Psalm 88 is the darkest and most notorious of all the psalms of lament because it's the only one without a turning point.[2] It's the only one that remains bleak from beginning to end. In fact, the last word of the psalm is "darkness" (Psalm 88:18). We're to understand that the psalmist finished his prayer-song while still inhabiting darkness. Some Bible scholars have struggled with its inclusion in the canon of holy writ because it doesn't move from a place of suffering to a place of hope. Thus, it appears unscriptural—blasphemous even.

But I love Psalm 88. I love it because it's honest. It's how the writer was feeling in a terrible season of life that was clearly painful and seemingly hopeless. But you know what else Psalm 88 shows us? Besides being gut-level honest with God, Psalm 88 shows us a soul that continues to talk to God even though his circumstances don't give him any reason to have hope.

> O LORD, God of my salvation, I cry out day and night before you. Let my prayer come before you; incline your ear to my cry! For my soul is full of troubles, and my life draws near to Sheol. (Psalm 88:1-3)

We don't know the particulars of this psalmist's situation, but we do know he hasn't stopped believing in God. He hasn't let his circumstances cast a pall of doubt over his faith. He still believes God is real and has the power to save him, so he continues to pray.

> Every day I call upon you, O LORD; I spread out my hands to you. (Psalm 88:9b)

Have you ever been in a season when everything felt hopeless? Have you ever despaired of finding a glimmer of light in the midst of total darkness?

If you have, then you know. You know how hard it is to face the unknown. Perhaps you're there now. In a long dark night of your own. Wanting to pray. Wanting to talk to God. But not sure if he's listening. Or if he even cares. If that's where you are right now, I want you to know you're not alone.

If there's one thing Psalm 88 teaches us, it's that we can still talk to God, even when we're struggling to find any kind of hope in our circumstances.

> But I, O Lord, cry to you; in the morning my prayer comes before you. (Psalm 88:13)

For me, I laid in that hospital in darkness, tethered to a bed with tubes and needles and questions. I didn't know what my life would look like going forward, but in that moment, I figured I could either stew in the unknown or I could talk to the One Person who did know. So, I prayed while waiting for morning.

In many ways, we're all waiting for morning, through a long night of sorrow, for our Bridegroom to come.

As promised, my husband arrived at 4:00 AM. Boy, did he have a story to share! He filled me in on everything that had transpired the three days I was in a coma. And I think one day our prayers will be the same. We'll sit in God's presence, and he'll tell us everything that was happening in the heavenlies while we were travailing here on this broken planet.

Because, as promised, our Bridegroom will return for us. Only we don't know the day or time. Until then, we each have our own crosses to carry and our own rocky paths to sojourn. In many ways, we're all waiting for morning, through a long night of sorrow, for our Bridegroom to come (John 3:29). Jesus is the Morning Star (Revelation 22:16), and he has promised to return, to make all things new (Revelation 21:5).

And while we wait, we can pray. That's my hope for this book. No matter what kind of season you find yourself in right now—whether life is rolling along pretty well, or life is feeling like a Psalm 88 level of despair—I want this book to be an invitation for us to pray, and we'll dive into the details a little more in the following chapter.

Shalom.

Gracious Father,
We cannot claim to understand
why some things happen as they do,
but we do know we can trust in you.
And when our trust begins to falter,
under the weight of everything we carry,
we pray you hold us fast through the night.
Help us to cling to you until morning.
In the name of Jesus, we pray. Amen.

(Psalm 139:10; Psalm 30:5)

TRUTHS TO REMEMBER

☀ God invites us to talk with him in prayer.

☀ It's okay if we're struggling to find hope in a season of deep disappointment and heartache, for that can become the starting point for prayer.

☀ Our suffering in this lifetime has an expiration date. Christ, our Bridegroom, will return for us one day.

CHAPTER 2

The Language of Prayer

"The words of the Lord are pure words, like silver refined in a furnace on the ground, purified seven times."

Psalm 12:6

God wants us to talk with him. If it weren't so, then we wouldn't see so many instances in the Bible when God asked someone a question. His questions weren't always rhetorical either. God already knew the answers to his own questions, but he genuinely wanted to engage in conversation with his beloved creation.[3]

> [In the garden of Eden,] the LORD God called to the man [Adam] and said to him, "Where are you?" (Genesis 3:9)

> [From the burning bush,] the LORD said to him [Moses], "What is that in your hand?" (Exodus 4:2a)

> [When Elijah was hiding in a cave,] the LORD came to him, and he said to him, "What are you doing here, Elijah?" (1 Kings 19:9b)

God knew exactly where Adam was. He knew precisely what Moses held in his hand. And he knew definitively why Elijah was in that cave. In each scenario, God wanted to talk, and Jesus continued this same pattern of question-asking during his earthly life and ministry as well.

> [When the storm raged and the disciples feared for their lives, Jesus] said to them, "Why are you afraid, O you of little faith?" (Matthew 8:26a)

> [When teaching a large crowd], Jesus said to them, "How many loaves do you have?" (Matthew 15:34a)

> [After Lazarus had died, Jesus] said, "Where have you laid him?" (John 11:34a)

Again, Jesus knew the answers, but he repeatedly invited others to converse with him. He wanted to draw them out so he could minister to them. You'll also notice that in many of these instances of inquiry, something miraculous was about to happen. Both then and now, God wants us to come to him with our thoughts, our needs, our hurts, and even our questions. God loves it when we talk to him, and that's simply what prayer is: talking with God.

If someone had asked me a decade ago to write a book on prayer, I might have demurred or muttered something along the lines of, "I really don't think I'm qualified." On the surface such a claim might be considered a sign of humility, or perhaps feigned humility, but still today I'm tempted to say the same.

Now, if someone were to ask me to write or teach on a literary work, I might agree since that's my background. The Bible, of course, is the only Book with living words, and it's my favorite Book to teach.

But prayer?

I've never considered myself a prayer warrior. Over the years I have, indeed, known women I considered to be genuine souls devoted to prayer. Whenever they prayed, I sensed something different in their prayers—something I knew I didn't have when I prayed.

Nevertheless, whether we believe ourselves to be particularly gifted in prayer or not, prayer is something we're called to do as followers of Christ. For instance, I've never considered myself a very good cook. And yet, every single day my family would peskily want something for dinner. Thus, despite my inept training in all culinary endeavors, I set about the task of learning how to feed my people without always going through a nearby drive-thru.

I bought recipe books before there was an Internet where you could download recipes for free, and through much trial and error (with great emphasis on the error part) I learned how to cook a few basics. From there my repertoire of meals expanded. Today, I'm a better cook than I used to be, and I love to have guests gather around my table.

And so it is with prayer.

I'm opening my door and inviting you to gather around my table. I want to share with you what I've learned as I've immersed myself in studying everything I can about prayer. The Psalter, of course, is the prayer book of the Bible. The Psalms are meant to be prayed or sang. They're one of God's most beautiful gifts to us because God has literally given us the words we can pray when we cannot think of the words we need to say.

Prayer is simply this: We breathe in God's Word and breathe out our prayers.

Prayer, I've learned, is simply this: We breathe in God's Word and breathe out our prayers.

Basically, the more we immerse ourselves in the language of the Bible, which is inspired by God the Spirit, the more easily we can converse with God who is Spirit (John 4:24). I'm hardly the first to recognize the Bible as the source of our prayers, but it's a timeless truth that never wears out. When we pray while reading the biblical text, "the Spirit of God will use the Word of God to help the people of God pray increasingly according to the will of God."[4] And when we pray, we certainly want to pray according to God's will.

If you type "books on prayer" in Amazon's search bar, over ten thousand possible results pop up. Solomon was right when he said the making of books has no end (Ecclesiastes 12:12). Do we really need another book on prayer?

Some of the books I've read on prayer were helpful and enlightening, but others were lengthy tomes in academic prose and dry tones. Shouldn't prayer be something alive and fresh and vital? Besides, when Jesus taught his disciples to pray, he did so in four sentences. At least, that's how it's translated into English. So, the brevity of this book is deliberate. It's not meant to be a wordy theological treatise on the subject of prayer, although I do aim to be theologically sound. I simply wish to impart the best of what I've gleaned over the years.

This little book on prayer is divided into three parts. Part One is an invitation for us to become people of prayer—people like Esther and Eunice, Hannah and Huldah. It's an echo of God the Father inviting us to commune with him in prayer. Part Two is an exploration of the most essential principles of prayer. It's a closer look at the teaching God the Son gave the disciples on how to pray. Part Three is more of a hands-on workshop, with prayers we can pray together, because I've noticed my own tendency to continue reading *about* prayer, rather than actually praying. So, instead of merely talking *about* prayer, as if we're dissecting a corpse for examination, I want us to pray. It's my prayer that God the Spirit would be at work here on these pages. The prayers in Part Three follow the pattern Jesus set forth, and they're steeped in God's Word; you'll notice the Scripture references within each prayer when appropriate.

No matter what our prior experiences with prayer may be, whether we have struggled to know how to pray for more than two minutes or have enjoyed long sessions of fellowship with God through prayer, we can always grow deeper in our prayer lives. This is my prayer for us: May this little book be a quiet beginning to a deepening prayer life for all who desire it.

Gracious Father,
You alone have the words of life.
You are the Word made flesh,
so we look to you in prayer.
Help us to know you more through your Word,
for your Word is sure and right and pure.
When we struggle to know what to say,
we know you understand us anyway.
For you understand all things,
as you hold all things together in your hands.
In the name of Jesus, we pray. Amen.

(John 6:68; John 1:14; Psalm 19:7-9;
Psalm 139:4; Colossians 1:17)

TRUTHS TO REMEMBER

* As followers of Christ, we are called to pray.

* The language of prayer is the language of the Bible.

* God gave us the psalms to pray when we're struggling to find our own words to say.

CHAPTER 3

The Imperishable Beauty of a Praying Person

"I am reminded of your sincere faith, a faith that dwelt first in your grandmother Lois and your mother Eunice and now, I am sure, dwells in you as well."

2 Timothy 1:5

As I left the grocery store with a bag in each arm, I passed the buckets of flowers and roses—all of them wilting a bit in the summer heat as they waited for some passerby to pause and notice their beauty, perhaps even take them home. The lavender roses drew my attention. I don't see that particular hue as often as I see red or pink roses, and something in me made me stop to appreciate their unique color. Upon closer inspection, I noticed the turned edges of the petals, fraying with age, and I thought to myself: *Me too, my friend, me too.*

After five decades of living, I've officially transitioned into that season of life typically called an empty nest. In my experience there are two kinds of empty nesters. The first kind of empty nester feels somewhat lost and adrift for a time, wondering what to do next in life. The second kind of empty nester embraces the new season with zeal, seeing it as a fresh start to something new and exciting, perhaps with more time to enjoy some of the ventures that may have been previously postponed.

When I became an empty nester, I was the latter. After my husband and I moved our youngest child into his college dorm, a fresh fervor for the future filled me. Instead of calling my home an empty nest, I called it a quiet nest. And motherhood doesn't end with a quiet nest; it simply changes.

While driving away from my son's college campus, I knew with absolute surety how my role as a mom would change. Instead of the dailyness of motherhood—with little ones underfoot or with teenagers and their crazy schedules to coordinate—I would settle into a new season where my primary job as a mom would look more like prayer. With my kids becoming adults, I wanted to commit myself to praying for them in new ways. Sure, I had always prayed for them. Even before they were born, I prayed for them. But prayer with little kids often looked like a tired mom pushing a double stroller in front of her while dragging a shopping cart behind her. Some of those days were spent praying for a way to make it through the day. Now I could pray with more focus. My days lay open before me.

About this time, Nikki Haley, a former governor of South Carolina, became a presidential candidate. In response to her candidacy, a popular news anchor went viral for saying she was "past her prime."[5] The news story got my attention because Nikki Haley was 51 years old at the time. Just a year older than me. Naturally, the news anchor's comments caused an uproar. Did he mean she was past her prime in terms of a woman's reproductive years? But he doubled down, and with a shrug of his shoulders he said to Google it, as if Google is the final authority on all matters. He was confident Google would confirm that women are in their prime when they're in their 20s and 30s, maybe 40s. But 50? That was clearly past the limit.

I had just turned 50 when his comment went viral, and I heard the world declare me past my prime, washed up, useless. Within days, of course, the news anchor issued the standard apology that publicists write for famous people who say dumb things. Then he got fired. But I kept thinking about this message women hear, over and over, and not just from a silly news anchor on television. Society tells women that our worth is directly tied to how sexy we appear to men. It's a lie, of course, but we see so many women believing this lie and it's eating them inside.

But God tells a different story. God says a woman's beauty is imperishable, and it comes from a gentle and quiet spirit (1 Peter 3:3-6). He says it about men too. When choosing David to be king, God told the prophet Samuel that people look at outward appearances, but God looks at the heart. God chose David because of his heart (1 Samuel 16:7).

This isn't some namby-pamby nonsense about having a good personality either. The Bible is clear that while we're encased in this flesh, our bodies are wasting away (2 Corinthians 4:16). Growing old is no joke, and the world isn't kind to older folk. But as long we we're alive and breathing, we have a purpose for being here (Ephesians 2:8-10). God has given each of us an assignment in our own contexts, and for all of us, we are called to pray, not only for ourselves, but also for others (Ephesians 6:16-18).

So, I see those lavender roses and their wilting edges, and I know their time is limited, just as time is limited for all of us. Moses said the span of our years are 70, maybe 80, if we're fortunate (Psalm 90:10). When we're young, we're convinced the decades lay stretched out before us, like an infinite ocean of time. But oceans are bound by sand and rocks, and the sand in everyone's hourglass continues to slip through, grain by grain. Our lives are but a "mist that appears for a little while and then vanishes" (James 4:14).

So, we must ask ourselves: *What do we want to do with the time we have? What difference do we want to make in the lives of our loved ones?*

Maybe you're fraying a little at the edges too, but you're still you, and if you're still here, it's because you've got something to do.

For me, I knew I wanted to pray for my adult kids. Of the different kinds of prayer—praise, lament, petition, confession, intercession, and thanksgiving—I knew I wanted to invest myself specifically in intercession. Not only for my kids, but for my friends' kids too, as well as for family members who are far from God.

Maybe you can relate to those cut lavender roses on a summer day, standing in opposition to the heat around them. Maybe you're fraying a little at the edges too, but you're still you, and if you're still here, it's because you've got something to do. The world may see "a woman past her prime," but the Bible affirms, again and again, the power of a praying woman.

Esther prayed. Hannah prayed. Anna prayed. Mary prayed. Lydia prayed. And so many more.

In his letter to Timothy, Paul lauded the faith of his mother Eunice and grandmother Lois (2 Timothy 1:5). It's notable that Paul didn't mention Timothy's dad, who was not a Hebrew (Luke told us this in Acts 16:1); rather, Paul mentioned his Hebrew mom and grandma because they were the ones who first taught Timothy the Scriptures. They were the ones who prayed over him as he grew.

I practically grew up at my grandma's house, and I don't have space to tell you all the ways my grandma impacted my life and my faith, but let me just say this: Grandmas make a huge difference. And Paul says as much in his letter to Timothy.

So, whether we have kids or not, whether we're young or not, we're never beyond being used in significant ways for God's kingdom. There is power in prayer.

Gracious Father,
We desire to commit ourselves to prayer,
and like the disciples we are asking you
to teach us to pray, afresh and anew today.
Help us to assume a posture of prayer
that is pleasing to you.
And when we are tempted to believe
the lies of the world, remind us
of the truth of your Word.
In the name of Jesus, we pray. Amen.

(Luke 11:1; Psalm 19:14; John 17:17)

TRUTHS TO REMEMBER

☀ When the world sees only the exterior, God sees the interior.

☀ Throughout history, the prayers of women around the world have had enormous influence.

☀ We are never too old or too anything to be rendered as ineffectual for God's kingdom.

CHAPTER 4

The Reason We Pray

"He drew me up from the pit of destruction, out of the miry bog, and set my feet upon a rock, making my steps secure."

Psalm 40:2

Whenever I write an article online or publish a book, I include my middle initial in my name. This began as a practical matter back in the early 2000s. Another "Denise Hughes" had already purchased that domain, so I had to include my middle initial *J* in order to carve out a digital space for myself. But since then, it has taken on a fuller meaning for me. Because now, every time I write something new and sign my name, I'm reminded where I'm from.

J is for Jeanine. I'm named after my drunk aunt, whose middle name was also Jeanine.

My family tree splits into two main branches. On one branch, we have the alcoholics, with a few drug addicts sprinkled in for added measure. On the other branch, we have the religious teetotalers, preferring instead to be "drunk in the Spirit."

My grandfather was a drunk—a mean, nasty one. When inebriated, he would beat up women and children, until one day he picked a fight, presumably, with someone his own size. A month before I was born, my grandfather's battered body was found stuffed into a steel drum on the docks of a nearby harbor. To this day, my grandfather's murder remains a mystery, but as I understand it, few tears were shed at his funeral.

Unfortunately, the talons of addiction had already passed from one generation to the next. My mother—the one member of her sibling group who didn't become an alcoholic—would sometimes get a call from the local town sheriff. One of her sisters was drunk, again, and she had a loaded shotgun aimed at her husband, again. Would my mom please come talk some sense into her sister?

Now, some family members felt he deserved to be shot. Nevertheless, my mom—the family's capable crisis manager—would drive to her sister's house and explain in a calm rational voice that if she shot her husband she would go to jail. Eventually, my aunt would relent, and the crisis-of-the-moment would pass.

With a potential second murder in the family thus averted, everyone at my house would resume life again, as if it was just another Thursday afternoon. That is, of course, until the next time one of my aunts needed my mom to rush to their rescue.

I've watched the same cycle of chaos continue with some of my cousins—now the third generation. I won't tell my cousins' tales, for their stories are their own to share. But the absolute destruction of alcoholism is the same story. Over and over again.

That could have been my path too. But as I said, there's another side to my family tree. In a strong reaction to the crazy-making of alcoholism, others in my family became religious teetotalers. This seemed far more sensible. Not to mention responsible. At the same time, I've seen how those of us on the sober side can easily sit in judgment. Like the older brother in the Parable of the Prodigal Son, it's easy to bask in one's own sense of self-righteousness (Luke 15:11-32). It's easy to point fingers at the weaknesses in other people, and after a while, it's easy to assume that oneself could never be capable of such travesties.

But if we live long enough, and are honest enough, we eventually come face to face with the depravity of our own sin. It may not look like the drunken chaos of my early family life, but all unrepentant sin leads to destruction.

So, there, in the middle of my name is the letter *J* for Jeanine—like a quiet reminder—pointing to the brokenness from which God rescued me. He lifted me from a miry pit, first from my family of origin, then from a pit of my own making, and he set my feet upon a firm foundation (Psalm 40:2). I can now agree with the psalmist: "The boundary lines have fallen for me in pleasant places" (Psalm 16:6).

To my aunt's credit, when she was sober, she was a delight to be around. She had a gift for making people laugh, and as a kid, I envied the way she could French braid my cousins' hair. I can testify to the beauty that mixes with the brokenness. It's important to remember this, too, because inside each of us is still the person God designed us to be.

With God, restoration of deep abiding brokenness is always possible; in fact, it's God's specialty.

We are not the sum-total of our worst decisions. While we are marred by sin, we are not defined by it. At least, we shouldn't be.

The *J* inside my name reminds me, not only of the brokenness from which I come, but also of the brokenness that remains, and the prayers that have yet to be answered. To be sure, I've witnessed God move in miraculous ways, but I've also endured the heartbreaking silence of God, wondering why he hasn't intervened in certain situations. Wondering why he hasn't come through on heartfelt petitions. Wondering why he hasn't rescued some of my loved ones (at least not yet). Perhaps you can relate.

Today, whenever I pray, I have before me the names of loved ones whose lives are still mired in brokenness. You probably do too. One thing I know for sure is this: The Lord isn't put off by the messiness of our lives. He doesn't turn up his nose at the stench of our own making. He remembers we are but dust (Psalm 103:14). He seeks to save those who are lost (Luke 19:10). And he invites us to partner with him by interceding on behalf of those who have yet to call him Lord (1 Corinthians 3:9). This is the reason we pray, knowing we're not the only ones who long to see our loved ones made whole (2 Peter 3:9).

> *Gracious Father,*
> *We are so thankful that you draw near*
> *to the brokenhearted and those crushed in spirit.*
> *You remember that we are but dust, and*
> *your deep desire is to see every soul saved.*
> *May our hearts align with yours*
> *as we pray for those we love.*
> *Lead us. Guide us. Teach us. Show us.*
> *For it is in your footsteps we want to follow.*
> *In the name of Jesus, we pray. Amen.*
>
> (Psalm 34:18; Psalm 103:14;
> Luke 19:10; Psalm 25:4-5)

TRUTHS TO REMEMBER

☀ My sin will be different from someone else's sin, but we're all in desperate need of God's saving grace.

☀ With God, restoration of deep abiding brokenness is always possible; in fact, it's God's specialty.

☀ We can partner with God in prayer as we intercede for our loved ones, for this is the reason we pray.

CHAPTER 5

The One True Mediator

"They made a calf in Horeb and worshiped a metal image. . . . Therefore [God] said he would destroy them—had not Moses, his chosen one, stood in the breach before him, to turn away his wrath from destroying them."

Psalm 106:19, 23

Throughout my adult life, wherever I've lived, I've joined the women at my local church in weekly Bible study. Today, I'm part of a local Bible study where a woman teaches our class each week. But twenty-five years ago, we'd watch the midweek teaching on a DVD with accompanying curriculum. Sometimes the DVD teachings were helpful, other times, not so much.

For one study, we spent several weeks on the topic of prayer. With our workbooks open and our pens in hand, we followed the video-recorded teaching. The teacher exposited the passage from Exodus, where Moses interceded on behalf of the people (Exodus 32:1-35). While Moses met with God on Mount Sinai, the people made a golden calf, worshiped it, and attributed their deliverance from Egypt to it. When Moses arrived, carrying two tablets of stone on which God had inscribed the Ten Commandments, he saw what the people were doing, and he threw the tablets to the ground. The broken tablets represented the broken laws the people of God were committing at that very moment.[6]

Moses then trekked back up Mount Sinai where God again announced his plan to annihilate the nation for their egregious sin (Exodus 32:30-32). Moses, however, pleaded with God on the people's behalf. He never excused their behavior, but he asked God to have mercy on them. Moses even offered his own life in place of theirs. God then relented and did not wipe out the entire nation of Israel (Exodus 32:33-35).

Most Bible scholars agree that this account is a classic picture of intercession.[7] But in my midweek Bible study all those years ago, the DVD teacher drew a particular application, saying that we also needed to intercede for our loved ones, just like Moses did. This was fine, but to drive the point home further, the DVD teacher also seemed to intimate that our loved ones might die if we don't intercede for them.

As I looked around the room, I could see women shifting in their seats, visibly uncomfortable. I saw a couple of older women silently staring at the screen with quiet tears streaming down their faces. When the DVD ended, silence pierced the room until one elderly widow stood up and said,

"Is that lady saying that my husband died because I didn't pray hard enough?"

The whole room erupted with a similar sentiment. Some women were angry. Others shook their heads in confusion. No one knew what to make of this teaching on intercessory prayer.

If this has ever happened to you, I am so sorry. There are certain teachings on prayer that appear to come from the Bible but then go awry, and I'll share with you what I shared with my friends that morning.

Moses was clearly interceding on behalf of the people who had sinned grievously against God, and God relented based on Moses's prayer. But we aren't supposed to see ourselves in the figure of Moses. Moses doesn't point to us. Moses points to Jesus. We're actually supposed to see ourselves in those who rebelled against God, and like those stiff-necked people, we too need a mediator between us and God. Moses was *a* mediator for the people in that specific time and place, but Jesus is *the* great Mediator for all people across all of time in every place (Hebrews 12:24).

Should we intercede like Moses for our loved ones? Yes, absolutely! Will they die if we somehow fail to pray long enough or pray in a certain way? No. This story in Exodus is not about condemning us as failures in prayer. This story is about foreshadowing the greatness of Jesus as our one true Mediator, the One who offered himself on the cross in our stead.

Jesus lives today to intercede for us (Hebrews 7:25). Which is really amazing to think about. The God of the universe, the Creator of all things, prays for us individually by name. He's praying right now even. For you. For me. And for our loved ones. This is reason aplenty to stop midsentence and give God praise!

Gracious Father,
We come before you
in awe of your grace.
You took our sin upon you
as you stood in our place.
Even now today you live to pray,
and we can never thank you enough or say
how much we love you and praise you.
You are our Lord and King, forever and always.
In the name of Jesus, we pray. Amen.

(Romans 5:6-8; Hebrews 7:25;
Revelation 19:16)

TRUTHS TO REMEMBER

☀ When reading the Bible, it's important to ask ourselves: What does this text, first and foremost, teach us about God?

☀ Scripture does give us examples of intercession, but the salvation of souls is not our job. Salvation belongs to our God.

☀ We have a Savior on the throne in heaven, praying for us today, and that is simply amazing.

CHAPTER 6

When the Answer Is No

"For all the promises of God find their Yes in him. That is why it is through him that we utter our Amen to God for his glory."

2 Corinthians 1:20

The story of the golden calf describes a time when Moses prayed on behalf of others, and God answered his prayer with a merciful yes. At another point in time, however, Moses prayed on behalf of himself, and God answered no. When those same stiff-necked people complained about water, God gave them water from a rock in the desert. The first time this happened, God told Moses to *strike* the rock (Exodus 17:6). He did and the water flowed. The second time, God told Moses to *speak* to the rock (Numbers 20:7-11). But Moses disobeyed. In his anger toward the complaining people, Moses struck the rock a second time. Yes, the water flowed, but as a consequence to his disobedience, God told Moses he would only live to see the Promised Land; he would not be allowed to enter it (Numbers 20:12).

For a long time, I read this story and thought: *Gee, God, aren't you being a tad harsh here? I mean, Moses was a good guy!*

But there is more to this story than meets the eye. That rock symbolized the coming Christ (1 Corinthians 10:1-4). In the first scenario, God instructed Moses to strike the rock. This signified that Christ too would be "struck" one day, and this is what happened on the cross at Calvary. In the second scenario, God instructed Moses to speak to the rock just as believers today can now come to the Rock of Christ and speak to him through prayer (Hebrews 4:16).

Moses messed up this picture when he struck the rock a second time. The sacrificial Lamb of God would need only to be struck once, not twice. Christ's payment with his blood on the cross was a once-and-for-all payment.

Still, for a long time, I considered God's punishment to Moses too harsh. Isn't God supposed to be a God of grace? But then I saw the grace in two ways.

Moments of Grace

The first moment of grace was when Jesus stood transfigured on a mountain with Peter, James, and John (Matthew 17:1-9). Two other men also appeared with Jesus: Moses and Elijah. Where was Moses standing? He was standing in the Promised Land with the Messiah in his glory! Friends, God is so gracious. You see, Moses's life wasn't over when he died. Moses is still alive today on the other side of eternity, and he *did* get to enter the Promised Land eventually. It was just a matter of timing. And that's not all.

The second outpouring of grace was more ongoing. Consider for a moment the possibility that God's "punishment" to Moses during his earthly life was really an act of mercy for the people of Israel. Because ever since the garden, the people of God were looking for the Promised Seed. After Adam and Eve sinned in Eden, God promised that a man would be born of a woman, and that man would defeat the Serpent once and for all.

> I will put enmity between you and the woman, and between your offspring and her offspring; he shall bruise your head, and you shall bruise his heel. (Genesis 3:15)

This is poetic imagery referring to the climax of history when Satan would strike Jesus on the cross, but then Jesus would defeat Satan when he rose again on the third day.

After God gave this promise in the garden, the people of God looked for the Promised Seed in every generation. This is really the story of the entire Old Testament. In story after story, they're basically asking one question: Is he the one? (Matthew 11:2-3).

Is Cain the one? No.

Is Noah the one? No.

Is Abraham the one? No.

Is Joseph the one? No.

Is Moses the one? No.

Is Samuel the one? No.

Is David the one? No.

Is Solomon the one? No.

Is Elijah the one? No.

Is Jesus the one? Yes!

If God had allowed Moses to enter the Promised Land during his earthly lifetime, the people of God might have thought Moses was the fulfillment of the Promised Seed. They might have mistaken Moses for the Messiah! After all, Moses was their deliverer. He led them out of slavery, out of Egypt. He gave them the law. He taught them how to live set apart from the nations around them. If Moses had also led them all the way into the Promised Land, the people might have been tempted to believe he was the one. And they would have been terribly wrong. Moses was *a* deliverer, but he was not *the* Deliverer. By preventing Moses from leading the people all the way into the Promised Land, God was protecting the people of Israel from making a terrible mistake. This is the grace of God on display.

When the answer to our prayer is no, it could be that the yes will come on the other side of eternity.

What we can learn from this story is this: Whenever we pray and the answer is "no," we can trust that God can see the bigger picture that we can't see. We can trust that—even when God doesn't answer a prayer the way we had hoped he would—God has a greater good in mind that he wants to accomplish. Perhaps his "no" is a quiet mercy in disguise, and we won't be able to understand it fully until we are face to face with Jesus for all eternity.

> *Gracious Father,*
> *We know there is so much we don't know.*
> *We recognize that you are in control,*
> *and you are orchestrating all events*
> *for all time to accomplish your good work.*
> *In you alone, all of your promises are Yes and Amen.*
> *And for every "unanswered prayer,"*
> *help us to trust in your unseen hand.*
> *In the name of Jesus, we pray. Amen.*
>
> (Isaiah 55:9; Philippians 1:6;
> 2 Corinthians 1:20)

TRUTHS TO REMEMBER

☀ Scripture points us to Jesus, the Living Water, who alone can satiate the deep thirst of our souls.

☀ When the answer to our prayer is no, it could be that the yes will come on the other side of eternity.

☀ And when the answer to our prayer is no, it could be a mercy in disguise, and we won't know the full story until we see Jesus face to face.

CHAPTER 7

The Ebb and Flow of Solitude and Community

*"When the righteous cry for help, the L*ord *hears . . ."*

Psalm 34:17a

There are two primary ways of praying. We can pray privately in solitude, or we can pray communally with others. Ideally, we do both.

Praying in Solitude

In his most famous sermon, Jesus prefaced his teaching on prayer with the admonition to pray in private, saying:

> And when you pray, you must not be like the hypocrites. For they love to stand and pray in the synagogues and at the street corners, that they may be seen by others. Truly, I say to you, they have received their reward. But when you pray, go into your room and shut the door and

pray to your Father who is in secret. And your Father who sees in secret will reward you. (Matthew 6:5-6)

In other words, God isn't impressed when we try to make an impression on other people with a spiritual performance. When our hearts' motivation is to be seen by others as super spiritual, God says he won't bless that kind of prayer. But when we pray in private, seeking only the Father, God honors this kind of prayer.

During his earthly ministry, Jesus modeled for us the importance of solitude and prayer.

[T]he report about him [Jesus] went abroad, and great crowds gathered to hear him and to be healed of their infirmities. But he would withdraw to desolate places and pray. (Luke 5:15b-16)

Times of solitude are necessary in the life of faith. It allows us to withdraw from the clamorous demands of the world and quiet the noise that surrounds us. It enables us to tune our hearts to the Spirit as he speaks to us through his Word. And it provides us the time and space we need to pour out our hearts to the Father in prayer.

After a time of solitude and prayer, however, we then return to our loved ones, our neighbors, our coworkers, and our church family. And it's appropriate to pray alongside a community of faith as well.

Praying in Community

Whether people admit it or not, I suspect most people love the part in the Bible where Jesus made a scene and angrily overturned the tables in the temple (Matthew 21:12-13). He was mad and for a good reason; the house of God had been turned into a marketplace. What we love about this portion of text is that we get to see the human side of Jesus. It just makes us feel better knowing he had some strong words to say too.

I've heard plenty of sermons where this passage was used to draw our attention to the fact that righteous anger is acceptable in God's sight. But far fewer times have I heard this passage used to illustrate what Jesus said is the primary purpose for the house of God. Jesus said:

> It is written, "My house shall be called a house of prayer,"
> but you make it a den of robbers. (Matthew 21:13b)

A house of prayer. The place where people gather to hear the Scriptures read aloud and taught should also be a place where people gather to pray. Indeed, if we want to learn how to pray, we must do so alongside veterans of prayer. I know this can be uncomfortable sometimes, especially when we're not accustomed to praying with a group of people.

The first time I attended a women's prayer meeting I was 22 years old, and the ladies spent more time sharing "prayer requests" than actually praying. (I'll share more about "prayer requests" a little later.) Once the praying finally commenced, I heard numerous shouts of "hallelujah!" and various persons "claiming victory." Needless to say, I found the experience gossipy and exhausting. I stopped attending this prayer meeting.

Years would pass before I'd brave the door to another prayer meeting. I still went to church and attended midweek Bible studies. I served in the church nursery, taught Sunday School, and led women's retreats. But prayer meetings? No thanks.

When I finally attempted another prayer meeting, I joined a few women before the start of our midweek Bible study. By this time, I had moved to another city and found a more gospel-centered church. Notably, the woman leading this prayer group did not ask for prayer requests. She simply stated that we would follow the popular acronym ACTS. We'd begin with Adoration, and as we felt led, we could pray out loud our words of praise for who God is. Then she would lead us into a few moments of silence when we could make our Confessions of sin to God. Next, she would lead us in a time of Thanksgiving where we'd proclaim aloud our gratitude for what God has done. Lastly, we would enter into a time of Supplication, praying for the women in our Bible study, praying for God's Word to be rightly proclaimed, praying for the leadership, and so forth.

I noticed something else about this prayer group. Whenever someone prayed a word of adoration or thanksgiving, they prayed using words and phrases I recognized from

Scripture. These women had clearly been serious students of the Bible for years, for the language of the Bible was evident in their prayers. I left that morning deeply blessed to be among women who loved God, loved his Word, and loved to pray. It's no coincidence, either, that these same women are some of the loveliest souls I've ever met.

Prayer in community, when done well, can be a beautiful thing.

Prayer in community, when done well, can be a beautiful thing.

A robust prayer life involves the ebb and flow of solitude and community. We pray alone in private; then we pray in community with fellow believers. In his classic book *Life Together*, Dietrich Bonhoeffer summed it up nicely, saying:

> Let him who cannot be alone beware of community. . . . Let him who is not in community beware of being alone. . . . Each by itself have profound perils and pitfalls. One who wants fellowship without solitude plunges into the void of words and feelings, and the one who seeks solitude without fellowship perishes in the abyss of vanity, self-infatuation and despair.[8]

Let us not fall into either ditch but stay on the path of God-honoring prayer.

Becoming People of Prayer

When it comes to prayer, we want to know *what* to say and *how* to say it, but before we get to the *what* and the *how* of prayer (which we'll discuss in Parts Two and Three), it's important to remember the *who*, the *why*, and the *when*.

Who are the people of prayer we want to surround us?

First, they're the ones who recognize their deep need for God. Whether they're going through a dark season or simply facing the regular pressures of daily life, people of prayer are those who know they're insufficient on their own. They need a Savior, a Deliverer, a Healer, a Redeemer. Second, they're people of all ages in all stages of life. Third, they desire to enter the presence of God on behalf of others, interceding for God's grace to be made real in the lives of their loved ones. Fourth, they know that sometimes a "no" is a mercy in disguise, and they trust that one day God will make his sovereign purposes clear. And lastly, but most importantly, they're people who immerse themselves in the language of prayer by saturating their hearts and minds in the text of the Bible, especially the psalms.

Why do we pray? And *when* do we start?

We pray because we want to know God on a deeper level, and we pray when we come to the end of ourselves. We pray when we recognize we're in a situation we can't fix on our own. We pray when no amount of money can solve the problem. We pray when no amount of medical knowledge can heal the illness. We pray when we've exhausted every other method we can think of. In short, we pray when we're desperate. And that's okay. It's really the best place to start.

> *Gracious Father,*
> *Thank you for inviting us*
> *to commune with you.*
> *Thank you for wanting*
> *to hear about our lives.*
> *We are so thankful that you hear*
> *the cries of your people.*
> *Help us to grow deeper in prayer*
> *that honors your name.*
> *May our prayers and our lives*
> *bring glory to your name.*
> *In the name of Jesus, we pray. Amen.*
>
> (Psalm 34:17; Psalm 115:1)

TRUTHS TO REMEMBER

☀ We never want to turn prayer into a public performance, for that is not honoring to God.

☀ Prayer in community, when done well, can be a beautiful thing.

☀ A place of recognized need is the best place to begin praying.

PART TWO

Principles

of

Prayer

CHAPTER 8

Prayer Begins with Praise

"Pray then like this: 'Our Father in heaven, hallowed be your name.'"

Matthew 6:9

The disciples asked Jesus to teach them how to pray, and Jesus gladly fulfilled their request by giving them the words we now call "The Lord's Prayer" (Luke 11:1-4). It's noteworthy that Jesus never taught his disciples how to preach, only how to pray.[9] Jesus expected his followers to pray, and if we're going to devote ourselves to prayer, it's wise that we lean in and listen to Jesus's instruction.

The Lord's Prayer is also referred to as the model prayer, for it's not solely intended to be a set of words we memorize and recite verbatim; rather, it's a model for us to follow. It's a form with distinct movements that we can adopt as we pray from our hearts.

As an English teacher, I've sat in department meetings and participated in numerous discussions on both the merits and demerits of the five-paragraph essay. On the plus side, it provides novice writers a basic format they can follow when learning to compose their thoughts into a structured and coherent piece of writing. It gives them a place to start and a direction to follow. On the minus side, the five-paragraph essay is limiting. Not every subject matter can be adequately squashed into five simple paragraphs. But it's a place to start, and with practice a growing writer can expand their thoughts beyond the basic parameters of the initial five paragraphs.

The analogy isn't perfect, but the model prayer is similar in that it also provides a pattern for people to follow when learning how to pray. This model prayer contains certain principles of prayer that are necessary, and we'll explore these principles in the following chapters along with a few other principles regarding prayer that are also found in the Bible.

Our Father in Heaven

As soon as we begin, we must contend with the pronoun *our*. Not *my* Father. But *our* Father. Right away we see the communal fellowship of the saints in action as they pray together. Part of us may like this idea of praying together, but another part of us may instinctively push back on the plurality of this prayer.

This is especially true when it comes to confession. I want only to confess *my* sins. I don't want to confess *our* sins. I don't want to be lumped together with other people who, for whatever reason, blew it. I want to be held accountable for my mistakes, not anyone else's. But this kind of individualistic autonomy is a modern way of thinking, and this isn't the pattern we find in Scripture. Again and again, we see intercessors in the Bible pleading on behalf of the people, using the pronoun *our.*

Three famous examples of this are known as the Great 9-9-9 Prayers found in Daniel 9, Ezra 9, and Nehemiah 9.[10] Notice how each of these men used the pronoun *our* when addressing God.

> O Lord, according to all your righteous acts, let your anger and your wrath turn away from your city Jerusalem, your holy hill, because for *our* sins, and for the iniquities of *our* fathers, Jerusalem and your people have become a byword among all who are around us. (Daniel 9:16, emphasis mine)

> O my God, I am ashamed and blush to lift my face to you, my God, for *our* iniquities have risen higher than *our* heads, and *our* guilt has mounted up to the heavens. (Ezra 9:6, emphasis mine)

> Now, therefore, *our* God, the great, the mighty, and the awesome God, who keeps covenant and steadfast love, let not all the hardship seem little to you that has come upon us . . . because of *our* sins. (Nehemiah 9:32, 37a, emphasis mine)

Amazingly, these three intercessors identified with the sins of the people even though they didn't commit those sins themselves!

The next word in the model prayer is *Father*. In churches today, it may seem commonplace to address God as *Father*, but in biblical times, this was most unusual. In the Old Testament, the people of Israel knew God as almighty and all-powerful. They knew him as the Maker and Sustainer of the universe. But to call someone *Father* is a term of close endearment, and this is exactly what Jesus wanted to communicate. God the Father wants to draw near to us, just as a good father enjoys the nearness of his children.

Initially, this would have come across to the disciples as too intimate, too familiar, but then Jesus completes the refrain: *Our Father in heaven*. This brings the appropriate tension back into balance. God is both near—as Father—and far—in heaven.[11] God is gracious, compassionate, and merciful (near), as well as holy, righteous, and just (far).

Hallowed Be Your Name

The entire Bible is about the holiness of God and our inability to be in God's presence due to our sinful nature. This is why Adam and Eve needed to leave Eden. It's why the Levitical priesthood offered sacrifices in the Tabernacle. It's why the people of Israel looked for the Promised Seed. And it's why we celebrate Jesus, the Lamb of God who takes away the sins of the world (John 1:29).

The word *hallowed* means holy. In the model prayer, Jesus taught us to begin with a rightful acknowledgment that God is holy, and his name is to be glorified above every name. We don't want to rush to our list of needs and wants without first recognizing who we're addressing. Pastor Jeremy Linneman put it this way:

> *When life gets sideways and we turn to God in desperate prayer, it's critical that we begin with the reality of who God is. He is holy.*

> If we begin with our problems and needs and forget who it is we're praying to, we may end up stuck in our problems and needs. To begin with God is to get ourselves in the best possible place to pour out our hearts.[12]

When life gets sideways and we turn to God in desperate prayer, it's critical that we begin with the reality of who God is. He is holy. *Our Father in heaven, hallowed be your name.*

People have asked me if the coma I experienced was medically induced. It wasn't. The blood clot in my brain wouldn't allow the blood to leave my brain and flow to the rest of my body, so the blood kept pooling inside my skull with intensified swelling until I finally slipped into unconsciousness and stopped breathing.

When I woke up in the Intensive Care Unit (ICU) on the third day, I noticed I had large bruises near my armpits which was weird, so I asked my husband, "How come I have these bruises?"

He got quiet, then said, "The doctors kept trying to wake you up. They pinched you there, saying it was a muscular pressure point. They called your name loudly and even shook you a little. But you wouldn't wake up. It was very distressing to watch. They came into your room every day to do this, and every time they left, I could tell they didn't have much hope for you. On the third day, after they did this to you again and left, I took your hand and started singing some of our favorite worship songs from the 1990s. After the first couple of songs, I started singing *Agnus Dei*, and as soon as I sang the words, 'Holy, Holy, are you Lord God, Almighty,' you opened your eyes. You looked right at me and nodded. You still had the tube in your throat at that point, but you were with me, and I knew in that moment you were going to be okay."[13]

When we reach the end of ourselves. When the doctors have tried everything. We can look to God. We can go to him with our desperate cries, and beginning with the holiness of who he is, he hears us.

Our Father in heaven, hallowed be your name.

Gracious Father,
You are holy, holy, holy,
and it is only because of the cross
that we can enter your presence.
Jesus, you bore our iniquities,
and by your wounds we are healed.
How can we ever stop worshiping you?
How can we ever stop shouting your praise?
For you alone are the God who saves,
the God who redeems, the God who heals.
May your name be glorified, forever and always.
In the name of Jesus, we pray. Amen.

(Revelation 4:8; Hebrews 10:19;
Isaiah 53:4-5; Psalm 34:1)

TRUTHS TO REMEMBER

☀ In the pronoun *our,* we see the communal fellowship of the saints in action as they pray together.

☀ God is both near—as Father—and far—in heaven.

☀ When we pray, we begin by praising God and proclaiming the truth of who he is: God is holy.

CHAPTER 9

Prayer Includes Lament and Surrender

*"Your kingdom come, your will be done, on
earth as it is in heaven."*

Matthew 6:10

Every November our culture inundates us with memes and articles about being grateful. I confess I have a complicated relationship with worldly forms of gratitude. I deeply appreciate biblical gratitude, but I remain skeptical of digital gratitude, because on social media, gratitude typically gets reduced to a humblebrag and a hashtag. Which is why I appreciated an article at *The Wall Street Journal* titled, "The Case for Being Ungrateful," with the subtitle, "There's a dark side to gratitude."[14]

Whoa. A dark side to gratitude?

Written from a nonbeliever's perspective, this article described the gratitude industry—how the idea of gratitude has been turned into a retail franchise for monetary gain. From t-shirts to coffee mugs, we find this two-word dictum brandished everywhere: *Be grateful*. It's a booming industry. What's more, the article discussed the idea that "performative gratitude—compelling ourselves to be grateful when we're not—is a form of toxic positivity."[15] That phrase—performative gratitude—captures the essence of how the online world has turned the beauty of genuine biblical gratitude into an online performance.

Moments before Jesus taught the disciples how to pray, he warned them not to perform their acts of righteousness in front of others (Matthew 6:1). The Bible does, indeed, instruct us to be grateful, and the psalms are filled with expressions of gratitude. But when we look a little closer, we'll also notice how those biblical expressions of gratitude always turn our gaze toward the One who has saved us. Sure, we can be grateful for all those other little things, too, because every good and perfect gift is from the Father (James 1:17), but the highest form of gratitude will turn our focus toward the God who rescues and redeems and restores.

Does this mean we shouldn't ever express our gratitude in front of other people? Of course not. In that same sermon, Jesus also told us to let our light shine (Matthew 5:16). But we don't shine for the purpose of being seen; we shine because we're simply doing what God has called us to do, being who God has called us to be. And those same psalms that give plenty of ink to expressions of gratitude also give plenty of ink to expressions of lament.

The Biblical Case for an Un-Gratitude List

Yes, biblical lament is an actual thing. You can think of it as the Bible's un-gratitude list.

The psalms of lament show us, again and again, that we can come to God with our complaints. When pain and confusion reign in our hearts, we can pour out our hearts to God with raw honesty. Unfortunately, few of us in the church have been taught how to rightly lament before God.

In his book *Dark Clouds, Deep Mercy*, Mark Vroegop explained that biblical lament follows a pattern with four movements that are best understood as *turn* (to God), *complain*, *ask*, and *trust*.[16] For those not well-versed in the psalms, it might sound heretical to say it's okay to complain to God, but there's a difference between complaining *to* God and complaining *against* him. Lament leads us to the Father as we 1) turn to him in earnest prayer, 2) share with him the hurts and disappointments we're struggling with, 3) ask him to help us in our time of need, and then 4) express our desire to trust him with every detail of our lives.

The presence of grief does not automatically mean the absence of gratitude.

True hope begins with real honesty, and lament is the means by which we communicate our pain.

It's fine to make a list of the things we're grateful for, but it's also fine to make a list of the things we're struggling with—the situations we're rightly grieving—and then give that list to God, asking him to help us carry the burdens that are weighing us down. The presence of grief does not automatically mean the absence of gratitude. We are not "less than" for feeling grief, just as we are not "more than" if we can rattle off a lengthy gratitude list.[17]

You might say I have as much experience with lament as I do with gratitude. Perhaps you can relate, but it's also true that the degree to which we have known the depths of sorrow and lament is the degree to which we can know the heights of joy and gratitude.

Your Kingdom Come

When Jesus taught the disciples how to pray, he told them (and us) to say, "Your kingdom come." With this prayer, Jesus acknowledged the reality that God's kingdom in heaven is not yet fully consummated on earth. Until Christ our Bridegroom returns, we live on a broken planet marred by sin, and Jesus warned us that we'd experience suffering in this world (John 16:33).

Lament, then, is a helpful means of prayer as we navigate the heartaches of this life. And when we pray, "Your kingdom come," we're recognizing that not everything here on earth is as it should be, we're lamenting the heartaches this world brings, and we're saying to God that we want his kingdom, not our own.[18] With hope-filled expectation, we pray for and look forward to the day when Christ our King returns and makes his kingdom fully manifest on earth, when he heals all diseases and rights all wrongs and restores all brokenness. Until then, we also pray for God's kingdom to grow in our hearts as we live each day in obedience to God's expressed will.

Your Will Be Done, On Earth As It Is in Heaven

Why should we pray for God's will to be done? Isn't God's will always done?

Born in 1886, theologian Arthur Pink said the will of God is best understood in two ways. First, the will of God is "what God has purposed to do," and his will is always done.[19] Second, the will of God is "what God has commanded us to do," and this, of course, is not always done, for we live in a broken, sin-filled world.[20]

So, when we pray, "Your will be done," we're asking for God's strength and grace to help us obey his revealed will in his Word and follow his commands. It's a prayer of surrender—where we intentionally subordinate our wills to God's will. With this prayer, we recognize our struggle with self-will and our need for the power of the Holy Spirit to assist us in our daily living.

This prayer of surrender isn't easy though. When Jesus prayed in the garden of Gethsemane, he asked, "Father, if you are willing, remove this cup from me. Nevertheless, not my will, but yours, be done" (Luke 22:42). God the Father answered his prayer with a no. The cross was the only way.

To pray, "Your will be done," isn't an easy-breezy prayer. It might take everything we've got. Luke reported that while Jesus prayed this prayer, "his sweat became like great drops of blood" (Luke 22:44). Even God in the flesh struggled with this prayer. But still he prayed it. Then he lived it.

Prayers of lament and surrender are among the most difficult prayers to pray. It means we're acknowledging that life on this earth isn't operating how it was originally designed to work, and we're struggling with something too heavy for us to carry on our own. But God not only hears these prayers, he also promises he's working in ways right now we may not be able to see.

In the meantime, we know God is collecting our tears in a bottle (Psalm 56:8). And when our Bridegroom returns for us, he will wipe every tear from our eyes (Revelation 21:4). Until then, we pray:

Your kingdom come, your will be done, on earth as it is in heaven.

Gracious Father,
You are the Lord who restores us,
bringing the long-awaited rains,
like streams in the desert.
While we sow in tears through long dark nights,
we trust you will bring a harvest of joy,
so while we are waiting for morning,
we look to you with hope,
knowing you will redeem and restore all things.
In the name of Jesus, we pray. Amen.

(Psalm 126:4-6)

TRUTHS TO REMEMBER

☀ The psalms of lament show us that we can come to God with our complaints.

☀ When we pray, "Your kingdom come," we're recognizing that not everything here on earth is as it should be, and we're praying for God's kingdom to grow in our hearts today, even while we wait for his return when he establishes his kingdom once and for all.

☀ When we pray, "Your will be done," we're surrendering to God's will for our lives, asking for his strength and grace to sustain us.

CHAPTER 10

Prayer Leads to Petition for Provision

"Give us this day our daily bread . . ."

Matthew 6:11

The model prayer that Jesus taught the disciples has seven petitions. The first three petitions rightly place our focus on God the Father, emphasizing his name, his kingdom, and his will.[21]

- ☀ Hallowed be *your name.*
- ☀ *Your kingdom* come.
- ☀ *Your will* be done.

The model prayer then makes a shift. It graciously turns our attention from God to our needs.

- ☀ *Give us* this day our daily bread.
- ☀ *Forgive us* our debts.
- ☀ *Lead us* not into temptation.
- ☀ *Deliver us* from evil.

Give Us This Day

By asking for daily bread, this petition draws attention to our physical needs. The bread here represents more than our need for nourishment, it represents all of our material needs, like housing and clothing. God knows we have basic needs, and he wants to fulfill those needs. This prayer, then, serves to acknowledge our dependence on God for our every need.[22]

In North America, most of us probably aren't going without food. I'm embarrassed to admit how often I need to throw away food because we don't eat it fast enough and it goes bad. This was especially true once we became empty nesters. It took some time to adjust to buying fewer groceries and making meals for just two people. We had a lot of leftovers.

With this reality in view, "We must not let the availability of food trick us into thinking we are self-sufficient and do not need God to provide our daily needs."[23] We know we can drive to the store and buy more food when we need it, but this prayer for daily bread serves as a necessary reminder: God is the one who gives us the ability to work and provides us with our jobs. Our livelihoods are completely dependent upon God. He is the one who sustains us, so we pray, "Give us this day our daily bread."

Our Daily Bread

Jesus didn't instruct us to pray for enough bread to last a whole month or even a week. We're to pray for what we need today. This echoes the wilderness years when the Israelites wandered the desert for four decades and God provided manna each morning.[24] They needed to gather only what they could use that day. If they tried to save extra for the following day, it would go bad overnight (Exodus 16:1-36). Enough for today is the theme of this petition, underscoring once again our daily dependence upon God.

The plural pronoun *our* is present again for good reason. We're to pray not only for our own physical needs but also for the physical needs of others. And when we have ample supply in our own cupboards, we can look to meet the needs of our neighbors.

Praying for Our Physical Needs

When it comes to praying for our physical needs, we probably think more in terms of our physical health than our need for actual bread. Again, the psalms show us the appropriateness of praying for this. David prayed:

> O Lord my God, I cried to you for help, and you have healed me. (Psalm 30:2)

Other Bible versions, like the *New Living Translation*, render that word "healed" as "restored my health." David's healing, in this instance, was a physical healing from some ailment.

Soon after I woke up in the hospital, I started asking when I could go home. The intubation from being on a ventilator for three days had damaged my vocal cords, and my voice would need several months to heal, but other than that, I was ready to go home.

I understand all too well that not everyone gets this kind of happy ending to a medical trauma. If you've read my book *Deeper Waters*, then you know that when my oldest brother was 19, a car accident paralyzed him and put him in a wheelchair for the rest of his life.

Why do some people wake up in the hospital otherwise fine and others do not? Why does God restore some people physically but not others? Why me and not my brother? The discrepancy is maddening.

To this reality I can only say: I believe in the God of the first part of Hebrews chapter 11, and I also believe in the God of the second part of Hebrews chapter 11. In the first part, name after name is heralded as a person of great faith.

> By faith Abel offered to God a more acceptable sacrifice . . . By faith Enoch was taken up so that he should not see death . . . By faith Noah . . . constructed an ark . . . By faith Abraham obeyed . . . By faith Sarah herself received power to conceive. (Hebrews 11:4-11)

And the list of names goes on. This chapter in the Bible is often referred to as the Hall of Faith, recognizing the people of God who obeyed him and lived by a faith that was pleasing to him, but rarely do I hear anyone quote the latter part of the same chapter.

> Some were tortured, refusing to accept release, so that they might rise again to a better life. Others suffered mocking and flogging, and even chains and imprisonment. They were stoned, they were sawn in two, they were killed with the sword. They went about in skins of sheep and goats, destitute, afflicted, mistreated—of whom the world was not worthy—wandering about in deserts and mountains, and in dens and caves of the earth. (Hebrews 11:35b-38)

These aren't happy verses. No one wants *that* story to be their own. But Scripture is clear. The life of faith is not a guarantee against heartache and suffering. Some of God's cherished saints endured brutal endings—including God's own Son! And without a doubt each of us today know of dear loved ones who have suffered beyond their share. If there was a prayer we could pray to make all the suffering go away, we'd pray it. But a life of health and prosperity and ease is nowhere promised in the Bible.

When we read the whole of Scripture . . . we see the overarching story of redemption leading us toward the ultimate restoration.

Yes, we can rightly pray for our needs, even our physical needs. And, yes, God hears us. But as we've seen with Moses's prayer to enter the Promised Land and Jesus's prayer to avoid the cross, God doesn't always answer our prayers the way we sometimes want him to. But when we read the whole of Scripture, from Genesis to Revelation, we see the overarching story of redemption leading us toward the ultimate restoration.

Why do I serve a God who has allowed my brother to suffer his entire adult life?

Because I trust Jesus when he said, "[T]he last will be first, and the first last" (Matthew 20:16).

The life we know in this world is not all there is. There is another world, a better world, waiting for us on the other side of eternity. There, God will restore all things. And for those who have put their trust in Jesus, if they were considered "last" or "the least" here on this earth, they will forever be first in God's holy presence. Because God is holy and righteous and just.

Justice will reign. And that is why we pray while waiting for morning, while waiting for the sorrow of this long night to turn to joy.

In that same psalm, David proclaimed the most beautiful promise in Scripture:

You have turned for me my mourning into dancing.
(Psalm 30:11a)

That is the day we await. When the Bridegroom comes, and we gather for the great wedding feast. When there will be dancing and feasting with the Bread of heaven who has come to redeem and restore. And until that day comes, we pray each day in recognition of our complete dependence upon God:

Give us this day our daily bread.

Gracious Father,
Thank you that we can come to you
with our physical needs.
Even though you know what we need
before we even ask, we still
ask because we know
we are wholly dependent upon you.
We lift up your name in praise
because you are a good Father
who loves to provide for your children.
We look to you today with hopeful expectation,
knowing that you are coming again one day.
And on that day, we will rejoice with dancing.
In the name of Jesus, we pray. Amen.

(Psalm 139:4; James 1:17; Psalm 30:11)

TRUTHS TO REMEMBER

☀ God welcomes our prayers for our basic physical needs.

☀ When we pray for our physical needs, we pray only for enough for today, trusting God to provide.

☀ When our physical needs are met, we can become an instrument God uses to meet the physical needs of others.

CHAPTER 11

Prayer Requires Confession and Forgiveness

". . . and forgive us our debts, as we also have forgiven our debtors."

Matthew 6:12

Jesus prefaced his teaching on how to pray with the admonition to love our enemies and to pray for those who persecute us (Mathew 5:44). I don't think I have any enemies, but several years ago, in response to this teaching on loving our enemies and praying for them, I thought of a few people I didn't enjoy being around—people who had hurt me in some way. Sadly, every one of them came from one place: church.

Not a neighbor.

Not a coworker.

Not even a family member.

Nope. The people who had hurt me the most had come from the one place that is supposed to be a safe haven. Church. To be honest, I wasn't sure what to do with this realization. Discouragement seeped into my soul as the real enemy hissed: *Why bother going to church at all? Some of the people there are so hurtful.*

As I pondered this, feeling a bit befuddled, I remembered why I thought of these names in the first place. To pray. So, I did. For every name that came to mind. Then something changed. Verses came to mind, which gave me a new perspective, beginning with this one:

> For we do not wrestle against flesh and blood, but against the rulers, against the authorities, against the cosmic powers over this present darkness, against the spiritual forces of evil in the heavenly places. (Ephesians 6:12)

The real enemy is not sitting in a pew, four rows over. We must remember who the real enemy is and know that we are not left defenseless because the One who is in us is greater than the one who is in the world (1 John 4:4). So, on Sunday mornings, I began a new routine. Before going to church, I started praying for my "enemies"—those who had caused me pain. I began by asking God to help me forgive them, even when they hadn't acknowledged the hurt their actions had caused.

And Forgive Us Our Debts

The Bible says that unconfessed sin (Psalm 66:18) and withheld forgiveness (Mark 11:25) are two serious hindrances to our prayers, so it's not surprising that when Jesus taught the disciples how to pray, he included the need for both confession and forgiveness.

When we confess our sins and ask Jesus to be Lord of our lives, he forgives us (1 John 1:9). Our slate is clean. The psalmist proclaimed, "[A]s far as the east is from the west, so far does he remove our transgressions from us" (Psalm 103:12).

In the model prayer, though, Jesus instructed us to ask for forgiveness, presumably daily, just as we ask for our bread daily. Some see this as a contradiction, but one theologian explained it this way, "[W]hen we were converted and justified, we stood before God as Judge; here, in the disciples' model prayer, we stand before God as Father."[25] Yes, our sins have been forgiven—past, present, and future—but when we confess our daily sins, we're acknowledging once again that "the cross was necessary."[26] This daily prayer of confession is a humble recognition of our need for God's abundant grace.

As We Also Have Forgiven Our Debtors

Whole books have been written on the topic of forgiveness, but Jesus summed it up pretty well when he followed the model prayer with a brief commentary of his own:

> For if you forgive others their trespasses, your heavenly Father will also forgive you, but if you do not forgive others their trespasses, neither will your Father forgive your trespasses. (Matthew 6:14-15)

Warren Wiersbe put it like this, "[I]f we have truly experienced God's forgiveness, then we will have a readiness to forgive others."[27] But this is easier said than done. If we've spent any time on this earth at all, then we've undoubtedly been confronted with the need to forgive an offense, and sometimes the very idea of it gets stuck in our throats because the very nature of forgiveness means it's going to cost us.

When we forgive, we release the person who has wronged us, and we agree to pay the price of what their wrongdoing has cost us personally. We do not demand recompense. We voluntarily absorb the loss.[28] Timothy Keller said, "[Y]our forgiveness means now you bear the cost of what the man has done. . . . The cost may be in reputation or relationship or health or something else."[29] Peter understood this reality, too, which is why he asked Jesus, "Lord, how many times must I forgive my brother or sister who sins against me? As many as seven times?" (Matthew 18:21, CSB).

Peter thought this was a generous suggestion, but Jesus countered him, saying, "I tell you, not as many as seven . . . but seventy times seven" (Matthew 18:22, CSB). If we do the math, Jesus told us to forgive someone 490 times! And that number is figurative. It's to indicate that we're to forgive and keep forgiving. In his book *Reflections on the Psalms*, C.S. Lewis wrote:

> There is no use in talking as if forgiveness were easy. . . . For we find that the work of forgiveness has to be done over and over again. We forgive, we mortify our resentment; a week later some chain of thought carries us back to the original offence [sic] and we discover the old resentment blazing away as if nothing had been done about it at all. We need to forgive our brother [and sister] seventy times seven not only for 490 offences [sic] but for one offence [sic].[30]

In other words, the cost of forgiveness cannot always be paid in one installment. I wish it could. It would be so much easier if the act of forgiveness could be a one-and-done deal. Indeed, the act of forgiveness does release the debtor once and for all, but for the person paying the debt, the wrong is sometimes so deep and so costly that it will need to be paid in a series of installments. Every time something triggers our memory of a wrong done to us and we begin to feel the injustice of it all over again, we absorb more of the cost, and we remind ourselves that we've already forgiven the offense even while we recognize we're still paying the cost of it.

With time and grace and prayer, the hurts may lessen and our hearts may heal with the hope that one day we'll "be able to comfort those who are in any kind of affliction" with the same comfort that we've received from God (2 Corinthians 1:4, CSB).

Forgiveness is serious business, and it's required by God. But forgiveness doesn't mean we automatically reenter into a relationship with the offending party. Trust must first be rebuilt. In her book *I Forgive You*, Wendy Alsup wrote, "You can forgive the one who has harmed you, but that does not mean they will fully recognize the wrong they have done or repair in the ways that are right. Though you can release them from the place they hold in your mind, a fully reconciled relationship is not always possible."[31] Timothy Keller agreed with this principle, saying, "[U]ntil a person shows evidence of true change, we should not trust the person."[32] Trust takes time plus the evidence of true change.

Also, it's necessary to recognize some offenses are simply that: an unkind remark or a hurtful action. But some offenses may also be a crime. Forgiveness does not mean a criminal should not face the legal consequences of their crime. Arthur Pink reiterated this, saying, "If a fellow citizen is guilty of a crime and I do not report it, then I become an accessory to that crime. I thus betray a lack of love for him and for society."[33] With God's help, we can forgive an offense—even one as serious as a crime—but at the same time, it is also right to report a crime to the appropriate authorities.

When Jesus taught his disciples how to pray, he made it clear that we're to confess our sins and ask for forgiveness, and we're also to forgive others. Yes, people will still be hurtful. Even church people. But sometimes we, too, will be the ones who need forgiveness extended to us.

> *God uses broken people, including you and me, and he redeems our brokenness for his glory.*

Thankfully, I'm no longer in that season of experiencing church wounds, and I still believe the Church—the global community of believers—is God's chosen vessel. It's a broken vessel, to be sure, which is precisely the point. God uses broken people, including you and me, and he redeems our brokenness for his glory. And because we're broken people stumbling our way through this life, we must regularly pray:

And forgive us our debts, as we also have forgiven our debtors.

Gracious Father,
You know all things,
even the motives of our hearts.
We ask that you reveal to us any
impure motives or untoward ways.
Forgive us of our sins, even the ones
we may not be aware of.
And help us to forgive others,
just as you have forgiven us.
We thank you for your abundant grace,
and the many ways you have
shown us your steadfast love.
In the name of Jesus, we pray. Amen.

(Psalm 139:4, 23-24; Psalm 66:20)

TRUTHS TO REMEMBER

☀ Unconfessed sin and withheld forgiveness are two serious hindrances to our prayers.

☀ The daily prayer of confession is a humble recognition of our need for God's abundant grace.

☀ When we forgive, we release the person who has wronged us, and we agree to pay the price of what their wrongdoing has cost us.

Prayer Seeks Deliverance and Protection

"And lead us not into temptation, but deliver us from evil."

Matthew 6:13

The Lord's Prayer rightly begins with our focus on God—his name, his kingdom, and his will. Then the prayer turns to our physical needs, asking for daily bread. This is closely followed by our most important spiritual need—the forgiveness of our sins. What comes next, then, is a logical progression; after asking for God's forgiveness and forgiving those who have wronged us, we then ask for God's help in keeping us from continuing in our sin. Because even though we're forgiven and saved by grace through faith, we still have a sinful nature and we still live in a sin-stained world, so our prayer for God's mighty hand to lead us is like "preventative medicine."[34]

83

And Lead Us Not into Temptation

The Bible, of course, tells us that God does not tempt us, but our sinful nature can incline us toward thoughts, words, and deeds that are not honoring to God (James 1:13-15). While we do have a real adversary, not every bad decision we make can be blamed on the devil. We are, as the old hymn says, "prone to wander" all by ourselves. Not only that, but we live in a fallen world with temptations and allurements all around us. It's the old trifecta of the flesh, the world, and the devil, and we need God's strength to overcome each.

And God is gracious, for he promised us:

No temptation has come upon you except what is common to humanity. But God is faithful; he will not allow you to be tempted beyond what you are able, but with the temptation he will also provide the way out so that you may be able to bear it. (1 Corinthians 10:13, CSB)

When temptation comes our way, we can trust that God will provide a means to overcome it, which is why we pray for God to lead us away from anything that could dishonor his holy name.

But Deliver Us from Evil

In Matthew 6:13, the *English Standard Version* says, "deliver us from evil," but other translations like the *Christian*

Standard Bible say, "deliver us from the evil one." This rendering is important for it discloses that we're not just dealing with some ambiguous sense of evil in the world. There are times when we're actually contending with the evil one or one of his lackeys—spiritual beings who are not mere folklore but who rejected God and now seek to cause destruction (Ephesians 6:11-13). Paul confirmed this in his letter to the Ephesians when he said:

> In all circumstances take up the shield of faith, with which you can extinguish all the flaming darts of *the evil one*; and take the helmet of salvation, and the sword of the Spirit, which is the word of God, praying at all times in the Spirit, with all prayer and supplication. (Ephesians 6:16-18a, emphasis mine)

The evil one and his followers are real, so Paul instructed us to pray at all times. Jesus modeled this for us when he prayed for the disciples, saying:

> I am not praying that you [Father] take them [the disciples] out of the world but that you protect them from *the evil one*. (John 17:15, CSB, emphasis mine)

Jesus himself experienced temptation from the evil one in the desert. After John baptized him, the Spirit drove Jesus into the desert where he fasted for 40 days and nights. During this time the evil one, Satan, tempted him, and Jesus refuted him every time by quoting Scripture (Matthew 4:1-11), which is a prime example of what Paul was talking about when he said the sword of the Spirit is the Word of God. We fight the evil one and all the forces of darkness, not with our fists raised but with our heads bowed, reading and proclaiming the truth of Scripture and praying for God's help in our time of need.

Now, when it comes to temptation, we might think Jesus had an advantage because he's God. But Jesus was also fully human, and he fought the evil one with the same means available to us: the Word of God, prayer, and fasting (which we'll talk about in the next chapter). We also mustn't ever forget that the evil one is a created being; he is powerful, but he is not equal to God in power. God alone is the Creator, and God alone is omnipotent and omniscient. Not only that, but Satan's time is limited, because the Bridegroom is coming.

While we do have an unseen spiritual enemy, it's also wise to remember these words by C.S. Lewis:

> There are two equal and opposite errors into which our race can fall about the devils. One is to disbelieve in their existence. The other is to believe, and to feel an excessive and unhealthy interest in them. They themselves are equally pleased by both errors, and hail a materialist or a magician with the same delight.[35]

Yes, there is darkness that converges in the unseen realm (Jude 1:6), but there is also light (1 John 1:5). Many verses in the Bible tell us there are angels ministering on behalf of God (Hebrews 1:14; Psalm 91:11; Daniel 10:12-14; Matthew 18:10; Luke 15:10; Revelation 14:6). And we mustn't ever forget that Jesus is the Light of the world (John 8:12).

Darkness is real. But so is Light. And Light overcomes darkness. Every time.

Darkness is real. But so is Light. And Light overcomes darkness. Every time. So, when we face trials and tribulations, we can take up the ancient prayers of the psalmist and say:

> I lift up my eyes to the hills. From where does my help come? My help comes from the LORD, who made heaven and earth. (Psalm 121:1-2)

And this…

> The LORD will keep you from all evil; he will keep your life. (Psalm 121:7)

Here, the psalmist recognized the truly all-powerful One who keeps us from evil, and that is why we pray:

> And lead us not into temptation, but deliver us from evil.

Gracious Father,
You are our refuge and our fortress,
and you alone can deliver us
from the snare of the fowler.
You command your angels
to guard us and bear us up.
And when we call to you in trouble,
you answer us and are with us.
You rescue us by your outstretched arm,
and you show us your salvation.
And we give you all the praise and glory.
In the name of Jesus, we pray. Amen.

(Psalm 91:2-3, 11, 15; Psalm 136:12)

TRUTHS TO REMEMBER

☀ We experience temptation from three places—our own sinful nature, the world, and the evil one—which is why we pray for God to lead us not into temptation, to keep us from dishonoring his holy name.

☀ The Bible is replete with examples of the evil one seeking to kill, steal, and destroy; the Bible is also replete with examples of people overcoming evil in the power of the Holy Spirit and the Word of God.

☀ Darkness is real. But so is Light. And Light overcomes darkness. Every time.

CHAPTER 13

Prayer Partners with Fasting

"So He [Jesus] said to them, 'This kind can come out by nothing but prayer and fasting."

Mark 9:29 (NKJV)

We can't talk about prayer and not talk about fasting. Throughout the Bible prayer and fasting go together. A biblical fast typically means to abstain from food. Today, the idea of fasting has broadened to include the idea of abstaining from any activity that may be fine in moderation but can become destructive in excess. For example, some people may choose to fast from binge-watching shows on Netflix, or they may participate in a social media fast.

Fasting has become popular in recent years, especially with wellness influencers on social media who encourage intermittent fasting for physical health reasons. But a spiritual fast is not the same thing as fasting for the sake of dieting. A spiritual fast must be for a spiritual purpose. In his book on spiritual disciplines, Donald Whitney offered the following reasons for a spiritual fast:[36]

- ☀ To strengthen our prayers

- ☀ To seek guidance from God

- ☀ To express grief over sin or a loss

- ☀ To seek God's protection

- ☀ To overcome temptation

These are a few of the many reasons people choose to fast. For our purposes here, we'll concern ourselves mainly with the idea that fasting strengthens our prayers. The Bible doesn't explicitly state *how* fasting strengthens our prayers, but it does give us many examples of God's people fasting and praying.

Moses fasted and prayed when he met with God on Mount Sinai (Exodus 34:28). David also fasted at different times, especially when facing a difficult circumstance (Psalm 35:13; 2 Samuel 12:16). Esther and all the Hebrew exiles fasted when they were facing extermination as a race (Esther 4:16). In the Great 9-9-9 Prayers mentioned earlier, all three intercessors—Daniel, Ezra, and Nehemiah—fasted in conjunction with their prayers (Daniel 9:3; Ezra 9:5; Nehemiah 9:1-2). Even the people of Nineveh fasted and prayed to express repentance after Jonah preached to them (Jonah 3:1-10). Jesus fasted and prayed the entire 40 days he was in the wilderness and faced temptation from the evil one (Matthew 4:1-2). And in the New Testament, the church at Antioch fasted and prayed (Acts 13:1-3). These are just a few examples, and there are many more.

Not only does the Bible give us many examples of prayer partnering with fasting, but Jesus also taught us how to fast. Right after he finished the Lord's Prayer, he then taught on fasting.

> And when you fast, do not look gloomy like the hypocrites, for they disfigure their faces that their fasting may be seen by others. Truly, I say to you, they have received their reward. But when you fast, anoint your head and wash your face, that your fasting may not be seen by others but by your Father who is in secret. And your Father who sees in secret will reward you. (Matthew 6:16-18)

Notice how Jesus didn't say "if you fast," but "when you fast." Jesus expected his followers to fast, but like his instructions on prayer, fasting should be done in secret and not for show. The disciples of John, however, noticed that Jesus's disciples didn't fast, so they asked him about it. Jesus answered them:

> Can the wedding guests mourn as long as the bridegroom is with them? The days will come when the bridegroom is taken away from them, and then they will fast. (Matthew 9:15)

Here again, Jesus used the metaphor of the Bridegroom, referring to himself. While we await his return and the great wedding feast, we are called to fast alongside our prayers. Without question, prayer partners with fasting.

What Fasting Does

The Bible clearly teaches that fasting is expected, and it gives many examples of people fasting and praying. But since it does not explain *how* fasting strengthens our prayers, an illustration by Andrew Murray proves helpful.

> Prayer is the one hand with which we grasp the invisible; fasting is the other with which we let loose and cast away the visible. . . . Prayer is the reaching out after God and the unseen; fasting is the letting go of all that is of the seen and temporal.[37]

With prayer, we're reaching out to an invisible and eternal God. With fasting, we're voluntarily choosing to let go of visible and temporal comforts.

With prayer, we're reaching out to an invisible and eternal God. With fasting, we're voluntarily choosing to let go of visible and temporal comforts.

Food is one of our most basic needs. It's why we pray, "Give us this day our daily bread." We cannot live for long without food, so when we fast—by abstaining from food for a limited duration of time—we're recognizing our finite nature as creatures. When we fast, we're acknowledging that we're not only physical beings but also spiritual beings, and just as we're dependent upon food for physical survival, we're dependent upon God for spiritual survival.

Fasting is a sure way to humble ourselves before God. When we fast, we see just how quickly a less-than-noble side of us emerges. When we're hungry, we easily become curt, irritable, and impatient. Fasting denies us the self-delusion that we are strong and capable on our own. Fasting also expresses our willingness to forego physical strength for spiritual strength. Again, Andrew Murray explained:

> We are creatures of the senses. Our mind is helped by what comes to us embodied in concrete form; fasting helps to express, to deepen, and to confirm our resolution that we are ready to sacrifice any-thing—to sacrifice ourselves to attain what we seek for the kingdom of God.[38]

Fasting is good and right when done with the purpose of seeking God and strengthening our prayers.

The Curious Case of the Missing Verse

Right after the transfiguration, Jesus descended the mountain and came upon the disciples and a crowd. A father had brought his son to the disciples and begged them to cast out the demon that was terrorizing his boy. Jesus had previously given the disciples authority to heal people and cast out demons, but this time they failed. The demon stubbornly refused to leave the boy. Jesus then drove out the demon and restored the boy to wholeness (Mark 9:14-27).

Later, the disciples asked Jesus why they couldn't cast out the demon. Jesus answered, "This kind can come out by nothing but prayer and fasting" (Mark 9:29, NKJV). Your Bible may have a footnote on this verse because some transcripts say "prayer" and others say, "prayer and fasting." The same thing occurs in Matthew's account of this same story.

In Matthew 17:21, Jesus said, "However, this kind does not go out except by prayer and fasting" (NKJV). Just for fun, put this book down for a moment and open your Bible to Matthew 17:21. Every Bible has a verse 20 and a verse 22, but some Bible translations omit verse 21. In its place is usually a tiny footnote, explaining that some of the earliest transcripts include verse 21 and some do not.

In either case, it's clear that some demons are stronger than others. The kind that tormented this boy, Jesus said, was so strong it could only be driven out by prayer, and in all likelihood, prayer *and* fasting. (For another biblical example of differing powers in the spiritual realm, see Daniel 10:1-14, but again, our God is greater.)

Our takeaway from this is the reality that fasting strengthens our prayers.

Fasting, however, is not a tool for manipulating God. It's not a means for getting what we want from the Almighty. Moreover, if our fasting is not accompanied by a life that's pleasing to God, then our fasting is in vain. This was Isaiah's point when the people complained that their fasting wasn't producing the results they wanted. Isaiah said:

> Behold, in the day of your fast you seek your own pleasure, and oppress all your workers. Behold, you fast only to quarrel and to fight and to hit with a wicked fist. Fasting like yours this day will not make your voice to be heard on high. (Isaiah 58:3b-4)

In other words, we can't merely fast and expect God to deliver whatever we ask. Our fasting must be accompanied by a life that honors God. While we may not be oppressing workers like Isaiah pointed out to the Israelites, I appreciate what Pastor Jeremy Linneman had to say about fasting:

> Fasting helps us discover those sneaky, socially acceptable sins that pile up bit by bit—the ones that we don't even realize weigh us down because we're so used to carrying them. . . . We might say the most pressing temptations for us are not the things that are purely wrong—rejecting the faith, drinking into drunkenness, viewing pornography. The biggest temptations for us are far more subtle; they're things that are good in moderation, but we go overboard—movies, shows, social media, caffeine, sugar, shopping.[39]

For me, I once fasted by giving up Mountain Dew. That may sound silly, but I don't drink coffee. So, my only source of caffeine was that ultra-sugary, highly caffeinated green soda. And the truth is, I was addicted to the stuff. I couldn't get through the day without my noontime Mountain Dew. And Paul's passage convicted me:

> 'All things are lawful for me,' but not all things are helpful. 'All things are lawful for me,' but I will not be dominated by anything. (1 Corinthians 6:12)

I was being dominated every day by my need for an afternoon-caffeine-pick-me-up. Fasting helped me lay down the thing that was, in a sense, controlling me.

Typically, a fast consists of giving up a meal for the sake of prayer. On some occasions, we may set aside a full day for fasting and prayer. Those hunger pangs, then, serve to remind us of why we're fasting in the first place. Typically, we determine ahead of time the spiritual purpose for a fast. Maybe we're seeking God's guidance on an important decision we need to make. Or maybe we're sensing a serious need to intercede for a loved one. Longer fasts usually extend to three days or maybe seven. Drinking water is commonly accepted during a fast.

When we do fast individually to strengthen our prayer lives, we want to follow Jesus's instructions and fast in secret. We don't want to announce our fasts online or on Sunday mornings when we're chatting with friends. There are times when our pastor may call a churchwide fast for a specific reason, but even then, we're to refrain from announcing our fasts in a public manner, like on social media.

Fasting and prayer go together. The one strengthens the other. It's a means God has ordained for us when we're serious about humbling ourselves and reaching after God.

Gracious Father,
Thank you for your promise
that when we seek you
with all of our hearts,
we will find you.
Help us not to fear a fast,
but help us when we do fast
to keep our focus on you
while we pray.
We love you, Lord.
In the name of Jesus, we pray. Amen.

(Jeremiah 29:13)

TRUTHS TO REMEMBER

※ Jesus didn't say "if you fast," but "when you fast." Jesus expected his followers to fast, and he taught us how to do it properly.

※ When we fast, we're acknowledging that we're not only physical beings but also spiritual beings, and just as we're dependent upon food for physical survival, we're dependent upon God for spiritual survival.

※ Fasting and prayer go together. The one strengthens the other. The Bible gives many examples of this.

CHAPTER 14

I Love Prayer, But Not Prayer Requests

". . . do not be anxious about anything, but in everything by prayer and supplication with thanksgiving let your requests be made known to God."

Philippians 4:6

As Christ followers, we're called to be people of prayer, and if prayer was ineffective, then the Spirit-inspired biblical text wouldn't give so many commands for God's people to pray (Matthew 6:5-8; Colossians 4:2; 1 Thessalonians 5:17).

At the same time, we also live in a sin-drenched, broken world. Which means a beautiful thing can sometimes get bent and turned into a not-so-beautiful thing. Unfortunately, this is what happens with some kinds of prayer requests. Most of my experience with prayer requests has occurred in the context of a small group from church or a local women's Bible study. Naturally, we want to pray for one another, but *how* we go about this is key.

Three Types of Problems with Prayer Requests

1. The first type of problem with a prayer request occurs when someone starts sharing and shows no sign of slowing down.

As a small group participant, I have watched more than one small group leader begin to sweat profusely because they don't know how to regain the floor and kindly interrupt someone who has been sharing their "prayer request" for a solid 30 minutes. Discernment and gentleness are required here because sometimes a person is in genuine need and that is what the small group is for. But more often than not, the rest of the group becomes a captive audience to one person's drama, and the self-disclosure turns into too much information (TMI) which makes everyone in the room uncomfortable. To avoid this kind of oversharing, I'll offer some suggestions in a moment.

2. The second type of problem with a prayer request is the opposite of the first problem; this happens when someone offers a prayer request about another person to avoid becoming vulnerable herself, which nullifies one of the gifts of gathering with God's people.

I cannot count how many times I've sat in a small group setting and heard someone make a prayer request on behalf of their neighbor's cousin's friend whose coworker's spouse has an illness. When sitting in a circle of friends, it can be tempting to give the impression that we have our acts together, that we don't have any pressing issues. It's also temping to present ourselves as ultra caring persons when we share other people's problems in a sympathetic manner. But this is image management—making ourselves look good while exposing other people's problems. When we do this, we forfeit the opportunity to allow the body of Christ to care for us.

3. The third type of problem with a prayer request—and the most damaging—occurs when someone makes a prayer request on behalf of another person without his or her direct permission, and it becomes gossip.

Too often the people being "prayed for" do not know their personal information is being shared—and sometimes that information isn't even accurate. Regardless of how "well meaning" someone may be, prayer requests can quickly become a source of gossip. Paul lists gossip alongside the sins of envy, murder, strife, deceit, and maliciousness (Romans 1:29). Paul reiterates the seriousness of gossip in other letters too (1 Timothy 5:13, 2 Thessalonians 3:11). Gossip is a serious offense against God and against others, and this goes directly against the two greatest commandments Jesus gave us—to love God and love others (Matthew 22:37-40).

In his book *A Long Obedience in the Same Direction*, Eugene Peterson described gossip as "exercising power instead of practicing love."[40] Gossip is a form of exercising power over and against another person. It's an elevation of self at the expense of another. It's a verbal demonstration of one's own position of strength in comparison to someone else's position of weakness. Gossip is exploitative—the antithesis of practicing love.

The best way to avoid this kind of problematic "prayer request" is that we simply don't make a prayer request on behalf of others without their direct permission. That word *direct* is important. Too often we think it's okay to share information because we saw it posted on Facebook, or we heard something from a family member. Or worse, we heard something from someone who heard something from a family member. Let's not reduce the beauty and the gift of intercessory prayer to base gossip.

A Remedy for Problematic Prayer Requests

The best remedy for these problems is to lay down some ground rules for prayer requests in our respective contexts. Whenever I lead a small group or a Bible study, I tell the women on the first day that I consider it a privilege for us to pray for one another. To do this with grace and wisdom, however, some guidelines are necessary.

※ Prayer requests are optional. There is no pressure for you to come up with a request every time we meet. You are always free to pass.

※ When sharing a prayer request, take care that it concerns you personally. Do not share requests on behalf of others, including family members. In this way, we can better care for each other as we walk alongside each other in this season. I recognize that we all know people who are in a season of need, and I encourage all of us to pray for them privately as the Lord leads us. The purpose of this group, however, is to help each other grow in our faith journeys, and we can do that better when we are devoting ourselves to praying for one another.

☀ If you have a prayer request, please write it down on the slip of paper provided and either check the box that says you want this request to stay between you and me or check the box that says it's okay to share this request with our group.

☀ All prayer requests shared with this group must stay with the group. Do not share any information about anyone in the group with anyone outside of the group. Keeping a confidence is crucial in order for us to grow in love and trust for one another.

These guidelines help establish a safe place for people to come together as they study the Bible and pray for one another.

In his letter to the Philippians, Paul said to let your requests be made known to God (Philippians 4:6). He didn't say to let your requests be made known in a Slack channel at work; rather, let your requests be made known to God.

There are times, of course, when it's appropriate to gather with God's people to pray. Jesus promised, "For where two or three are gathered in my name, there am I among them" (Matthew 18:20). When we need prayer, we should gather with those we are in close fellowship with, so we can pray together.

Intercessory prayer can be a beautiful gift of grace when done with wisdom and discretion.

Even Jesus demonstrated a time in the Garden of Gethsemane when he wanted his close friends praying with him. They didn't do this very well because they kept falling asleep, but the principle of gathering with God's people to pray remains true. You'll also notice that Jesus didn't ask the disciples to go out and gather a big crowd to pray; Jesus asked his disciples personally to pray with him. Just them. Together in the garden. Because they had been walking in close fellowship with one another for three years.

This is what the body of Christ is for, and this is why we need to be embedded in a local church body. But even there we must take care to handle the privilege of praying for one another with consideration and discretion, which is why the above guidelines are so important. Prayer is an amazing gift God has given us, and we want to preserve this extraordinary reality. God has invited us to commune with him through prayer. He has also invited us to intercede on behalf of others, and we want to do this with care and respect for everyone concerned.

Gracious Father,
Thank you for inviting us
into your presence through prayer.
Thank you that when we come to you
on behalf of others, you hear us.
Help us to grow in wisdom and grace
as we intercede for others.
Guide us as we pray for our
families and friends and neighbors.
May our words always be honoring
to you in all we say and do.
In the name of Jesus, we pray. Amen.

(Hebrews 4:16; Psalm 5:1; Psalm 19:14)

TRUTHS TO REMEMBER

☀ Intercessory prayer can be a beautiful gift of grace when done with wisdom and discretion.

☀ Sadly, some prayer requests can go awry and cause fellow believers a lot of unnecessary pain.

☀ Guidelines for intercessory prayer help establish a safe place for people to come together as they grow in their faith journeys.

Practices

of

Prayer

CHAPTER 15

A Prayer of Praise

"I will extol you, my God and King, and bless
your name forever and ever."

Psalm 145:1

For many of us, whenever we try to pray, we tend to say the same things over and over.[41] To pray for any length of time, then, becomes a challenge as we get stuck saying the same things. We get bored and give up. Then we believe ourselves to be failures when it comes to prayer, which is why Part Three of this book is different. A book on prayer mustn't merely talk *about* prayer; it must lead a person into the heart of prayer before a living God. That is the aim of this next section: to pray.

Throughout my adult life, prayer has taken four primary forms. One, as I read the Bible each day, I talk to God as I read, and I continue to be in conversation with God (quietly inside my mind) throughout the rest of the day. This is likely what Paul meant when he said to "pray without ceasing" (1 Thessalonians 5:17). Two, I keep a prayer journal, where I write out my prayers after I've spent time in the Word.

This helps me train my focus and not mentally drift toward my to-do list for the day. Three, sometimes a very short prayer is all I can muster: *Jesus, please help. Amen.* Four, I've memorized certain verses and pray them when appropriate. Here are a few I pray regularly:

- ☀ "Speak, LORD, for your servant is listening." (1 Samuel 3:9, NIV)

- ☀ "May these words of my mouth and this meditation of my heart be pleasing in your sight, LORD, my Rock and my Redeemer." (Psalm 19:14, NIV)

- ☀ "Search me, O God, and know my heart! Try me and know my thoughts! And see if there be any grievous way in me, and lead me in the way everlasting!" (Psalm 139:23-24)

In these four ways, prayer has been a part of my daily life since I was a teenager, but in recent years, I've sensed a call to delve deeper into the heart of God through prayer. That's what the following pages are about. By writing out the following prayers, I want to pray for longer stretches of time, and I want to invite my friends to join me.

Taken together as a whole, the following prayers exemplify the pattern Jesus set forth in his model prayer. They also follow the biblical language found in the psalms as well as other portions of Scripture (you'll see the many references).

Before diving in, however, you're encouraged to draw upon the principles of prayer we've previously discussed. First, find a place to pray in private (in solitude). Also, consider asking two or three friends to pray these prayers with you (in community). When you see *[our loved ones]* in the prayers below, insert the specific names of your loved ones and the names of your friends' loved ones. For example, when I pray these prayers, I insert the names of my kids and the names of my friends' kids, knowing that when they pray these prayers, they do the same. In this way, we are praying for each other's kids as well as our own.

Second, consider possibly fasting in conjunction with praying. This could mean giving up one meal each week to pray. Or maybe postpone the first meal of each day until after you've prayed. There may even be occasions when you feel led to fast an entire 24-hour period, to designate that time for prayer. There are no hard fast rules. (Pardon the pun.) We never want to turn fasting into a legalistic requirement. Simply ask God to lead you in this area.

Third, remember that you're never praying alone. Jesus lives today to intercede *for* you and *with* you (Hebrews 7:25). And the Holy Spirit dwells inside you and leads you in prayer as well (Romans 8:26-27).

> *You're never praying alone. Jesus lives today to intercede* for *you and* with *you.*

Lastly, we want to heed Jesus's instruction preceding the model prayer, when he said, "And when you pray, do not heap up empty phrases as the Gentiles do, for they think that they will be heard for their many words" (Matthew 6:7). In ancient times, godless people would perform their prayers before an audience with a plethora of fancy phrases, hoping to entice the gods to do their bidding based on their wordy prayers. But the real God of the universe isn't interested in a pretty performance. There's a difference between polish and power, and the power of a praying person isn't found in their wordiness as much as it's found in the sincerity of their hearts.

I confess that part of me was tempted to write these prayers in iambic pentameter. Wouldn't that be fun? But I don't want these prayers to be about lyrical language that wows us, for that would make the focus more about style than substance. When it comes to genuine prayer, the Bible exemplifies straightforward, honest conversation as best, so that's what you'll find here. Plain and simple words that come straight from the Bible itself.

My hope is that we'll grow in our prayer lives to the point where we can pray for extended periods of time, and it doesn't even feel like much time has passed at all.

The following prayers are not meant to be memorized and then repeated verbatim. Warren Wiersbe wisely pointed out that the "mere reciting of memorized prayers can be vain repetition."[42] Rather, the prayers that follow are to serve as a starting point—a way for us to engage the Scriptures in prayer as we move through each section of the model prayer. They're to help us participate in prayer for an extended length of time, maybe for the first time for many of us.

If prayed aloud, each of the following seven prayers will take approximately eight or nine minutes to pray, depending on how fast a person speaks. Thus, all seven prayers in Part Three combine for a full hour of prayer!

Following the Lord's lead in Matthew 6:9, when he began to pray by saying, "Our Father in heaven, hallowed be your name," we'll also begin with a prayer of praise and adoration, beginning with words from Scripture about Scripture, as well as some words drawn from the psalms, including Psalm 145, which is accurately called a Psalm of Praise.

If we happen to find ourselves in a season right now when praise is hard to find on our tongues, the following words by Michael Card are fitting:

> In his final warning to Pharoah before the plagues were to descend upon and devastate Egypt, Moses, speaking for God, says, 'Let my people go that they may worship me in the wilderness.' The goal of deliverance is always worship. . . . The object of their freedom was not simply their emancipation. The purpose was the worship of God. . . . True worship begins in the wilderness.[43]

And this . . .

> If, as you are reading this, you find yourself in the wilderness, realize that though you may not feel like it at the moment, you are in the very place where the Bible reveals that true worship can begin. If you're like me, you might also find that you have nothing to say from where you are, no words to articulate the depth of the dimensions of your hunger, thirst, disappointments, frustrations, guilt, or anger. If this is where you find yourself, then I would like to propose that you (along with me) are poised on the edge of a promising place.[44]

Maybe you're in the wilderness right now. Or maybe you're not. Wherever you are, you can worship God. But when we do worship God in the midst of difficult circumstances, we are bringing to him a genuine sacrifice of praise (Hebrews 13:15). Let's do that right now.

Gracious Father,

__We want to know you more__ . . . so we ask that you open the eyes of our hearts that we might behold the wonder and the glory and the immeasurable greatness of who you are (Ephesians 1:18-19). You are our Father, because you adopted us through your Son, and by the grace of Jesus Christ, we have redemption, the forgiveness of our transgressions, and *because the Spirit has sealed us, we now await with great hope the coming of your glory on that day when Christ our Bridegroom returns (Ephesians 1:5-7, 13-14). And while we wait for that glorious morning, we ask today that you teach us to pray (Luke 11:1).*

We praise you . . . *because you are our Father in heaven, yet you have also chosen to reveal yourself through your creation here on earth, for the skies proclaim your handiwork (Matthew 6:9; Psalm 19:1). We praise you because you are our Creator, for you spoke the world into existence, you fashioned the earth from a formless void, and from the very beginning of time, you did what you do best—you separated light from darkness, and you called it good (Genesis 1:1-4). You then filled the sea and land with creatures great and small, then you breathed life into all—all who walk on this earth (Isaiah 42:5). And now we are yours, because the world and all that is in it belong solely to you (Psalm 24:1). For you hung the moon and stars and gave us light to navigate the night (Psalm 8:3). And we praise you for the way you made the seasons to hint toward your promise of resurrection, for as long as this earth remains, the flush of summer will inevitably turn to the fading glory of autumn, and the barrenness of winter will eventually lead to the renewal of spring. And if we fail to recognize your fingerprints on all of creation and respond with shouts of praise, the stones will cry out in our stead (Luke 19:40).*

We praise you . . . because you are the Word made flesh. From the beginning of time the Word was there, and that Word is you (John 1:1). While the flowers of the field may bloom and then fade, your Word is eternal and will endure forever (Isaiah 40:8). You not only speak words of truth, you are truth (John 14:6). We can trust in your Word because it is like rain from heaven, watering the earth and bringing new life, and your Word carries with it a divine purpose that will never fail, for you will always accomplish your will through your Word, because every word from your mouth is destined to succeed; it will never return empty (Isaiah 55:10-11). Your Word is perfect and flawless; it is a shield for all who find refuge in you (Psalm 18:30). We praise you because your Word is alive and active; it can penetrate our souls and judge our thoughts and know our motives (Hebrews 4:12). We praise you because your Word is like a mirror that can reveal to us our true nature, so we ask that you help us to listen well to what Your Word says and then faithfully follow through on what it commands (James 1:22-25). For your Word is a lamp to our path, lighting the way while we walk according to your truth (Psalm 119:105).

We praise you . . . because you promise to bless those who hear your Word and obey it (Luke 11:28). Help us, Lord, by your grace, to hold fast to your teaching, because only the truth can set us free (John 8:31-32). May your Word dwell in us richly, taking root deeply in our souls (Colossians 3:16). Your Word is a shield that protects us and sustains us, and *we ask that you help us hide your Word in our hearts that we might not sin against you (Psalm 18:35-36; Psalm 119:11). We praise you because your Word gives knowledge and wisdom and understanding (Proverbs 2:6). For we know that apart from you, we can do nothing (John 15:5). Which is why we rejoice, knowing that as we believe you and follow you and immerse ourselves in the truth of your Word, rivers of living water will flow from within, for you are the God of life (John 7:38).*

*   ***We praise you . . .** for the totality of your greatness is unfathomable, unknowable, and unsearchable (Psalm 145:3). You are the Most High God who bends low to bless your people (Genesis 14:19) and promises to fulfill the purposes of your sons and daughters (Psalm 57:2). You are exalted over everything, over the heavens above and the earth below, and you are supreme over every living being (Psalm 97:9). You reign as King and no one can match your greatness or your glory; you are the King eternal and immortal, and every generation will declare your splendor and majesty (1 Timothy 1:17; Psalm 145:4-5). You are the King over all kings, for no one can match your power and might. Your kingdom will know no end, your reign will never wane, and your dominion will never cease (Psalm 145:13). We praise you because your greatness is matched only by your goodness. Which is why all glory comes from you and belongs to you. For you are Lord Almighty.*

We praise you . . . because you are gracious and merciful, again and again, slow to anger, amazingly so, and abounding in steadfast love (Exodus 34:6-7). From the highest heights of heaven, you deign to come to those who experience the lowest lows of earth. You do not recoil from sorrow and pain; rather, you hear the cries of your people and draw near to those who call (Psalm 145:18-19). You uphold those who fall and raise up those bowed low (Psalm 145:14). You preserve those who love you, and you open your hand to satisfy the hearts of your people (Psalm 145:16, 20). Thus, we live each day to praise your name and extol your greatness, to tell of your fame and proclaim your kindness (Psalm 145:2, 7). For you are good, so very good.

We praise you . . . because you are the God of grace. We acknowledge that we could never enter your presence by our own doing (Ephesians 2:8-9), for your name is hallowed because that is who you are, you are holy, and it is only by Christ's innocent blood, poured out on the cross, that we can now enter your presence in the throne room of heaven (Hebrews 4:16). We ask for boldness to tell your story and to share your mercy to a lost and hurting world. Help us to speak of your awesome deeds and to sing of your righteousness (Psalm 145:6-7). Help us to stand strong in our generation, because you are our sure foundation, and help us to make known to others who you really are (2 Timothy 2:19; Psalm 145:12). Help us to follow in your footsteps as we bring good news to the poor in spirit. We pray for [our loved ones], that you would soften their hearts and open their eyes that they might see the greatness and the goodness of who you are. We pray that [our loved ones] will come to realize that you are the King over every living thing, and we pray they will bow their hearts to you as their personal Lord and Savior. We pray that for every argument they might muster as a defense, that you would, by your grace and mercy, show them the truth, that they may receive your Word. For it is only when we live by the truth of who you are that we will know freedom, and it is for freedom that you came (Galatians 5:1). For all of this and more, we praise you and worship you and bless your holy name, today and forevermore (Psalm 145:21). In the name of Jesus, we pray, our Father in heaven, hallowed be your name. Amen.

CHAPTER 16

A Prayer of Lament

"My God, my God, why have you forsaken me? Why are you so far from saving me, from the words of my groaning?"

Psalm 22:1

I grew up in a prosperity gospel church where people were regularly hailed for going from "strength to strength." I can distinctly remember how we'd celebrate Palm Sunday one week with shouts of "Hosanna!" and then Easter Sunday the next week with shouts of "Hallelujah! Jesus is risen!"[45] Conspicuously missing from my early church life was any kind of discussion around Good Friday. A brief, honorary mention of the crucifixion would quickly defer to the victory of the resurrection. And if someone in the church experienced any kind of suffering, it was met with suspicion over a perceived lack of faith.

Thankfully, God in his kindness eventually led me to a Bible-based, gospel-centered church. The psalms of lament, of course, were never brought up in my younger years, so I didn't even know they existed until I purposed to read through the Bible, cover to cover. Imagine my surprise when I discovered people in the Bible expressing their hurt and complaining to God! I found their raw disclosures strangely comforting. Their words resonated with the reality of life in this broken world.

In his classic book *A Road Less Traveled,* Dr. M. Scott Peck defined mental health as "an ongoing process of dedication to reality at all costs."[46] Dedication to reality. I like that. His definition is from a secular viewpoint, but it holds merit. When people live in denial of reality—pretending things are fine when they are, in fact, very much not fine—they buckle a little more each day under the weight of self-deception. It's only a matter of time before the rug of denial gets pulled out from beneath them and the smack of reality confronts them head on.

The psalms of lament are like medicine for a hurting soul. They begin by acknowledging reality, naming the pain for what it is, and then asking God to intervene.

The psalms of lament, however, are like medicine for a hurting soul. They begin by acknowledging reality, naming the pain for what it is, and then asking God to intervene. The medicine may not taste good going down—because dedication to reality will cost us something—but in the long run, it works to heal us from the inside out. I owe much to Walter Brueggemann, whose commentary expressed the truth about biblical lament in our day:

It is no wonder that the church has intuitively avoided these psalms [of lament]. They lead us into dangerous acknowledgment of how life really is. They lead us into the presence of God where everything is not polite and civil. They cause us to think unthinkable thoughts and utter unutterable words.[47]

Here, he's speaking not only of prosperity gospel churches, but even some mainline evangelical ones. Sadly, some Bible-preaching churches have an unspoken regard for those who present themselves as happy, healthy, and put together. These churches may have an orthodox *professed theology*, but their *practiced theology* is more akin to a prosperity gospel lite. This may not be evident on a typical Sunday morning, but as soon as a church member undergoes a severe trial, the hurting person will sense other church members—even the leadership—distancing themselves to avoid the uncomfortable messiness of human suffering. This effectually leaves the hurting person more isolated than ever, but the psalms of lament don't turn us away, they invite us in. Again, Brueggemann said:

The use of these 'psalms of darkness' may be judged by the world to be *acts of unfaith and failure*, but for the trusting community, their use is *an act of bold faith*, albeit a transformed faith. It is an act of bold faith on the one hand, because it insists that the world must be experienced as it really is and not in some pretended way. On the other hand, it is bold because it insists that all such experiences of disorder are a proper subject for discourse with God. There is nothing out of bounds, nothing precluded or inappropriate.[48] (emphasis original)

God doesn't distance himself from us when we're hurting. That's actually when he draws near (Psalm 34:18). He welcomes every part of us, even the unseen parts that may be struggling under weighty circumstances. There is nothing we cannot bring to God. Everything is in play. Even the hard parts of life, which is why we pray for God's kingdom to come, and for his will to be done, on earth as it is in heaven (Matthew 6:10). So, we turn now to a prayer of lament (to grieve) and surrender (to yield), following the same language found in many of the psalms.

Gracious Father,

We turn to you today . . . *with hearts heavy under the weight of sorrow. While we know we can never fully understand the cost Jesus paid for us on the cross, we do, in our own small way, sometimes feel like we can relate to his cry, "My God, my God, why have you forsaken me?" (Matthew 27:46). For that is how we feel sometimes, when we cannot sense your nearness and cannot hear your voice. The questions swirl like a tempest inside us: Why are you so far away?*

Why do you refuse to answer our cries? Night after night, we find no rest! (Psalm 22:2). How long, Lord, will this go on? How long must we cry for your help? How long will you remain silent? (Habakkuk 1:2). Will you forget us forever? Will you continue to hide your face from us? Will this heartache ever cease? (Psalm 13:1-2). Nevertheless, we will not stop seeking your face. Day and night, hour after hour, we will look to you. Like the persistent widow in the story you told, we will keep coming to you with our needs; we will keep crying out for justice and mercy, for healing and restoration for us and [our loved ones] (Luke 18:1-8).

We confess to you today . . . with our souls in anguish, that we do not understand why some things have unfolded the way they have. We know you are in control of all things, for you hold all things together (Colossians 1:17), and you are the one who directs our steps (Jeremiah 10:23). We know you have promised never to leave us or forsake us, and you have told us in your Word not to be afraid or discouraged (Deuteronomy 31:8), but honestly, right now, we're struggling with deep discouragement. Life has not turned out the way we had hoped, but more than that, life has actually beat us up pretty hard. Like in the Parable of the Good Samaritan, we relate more to the person who was beaten and left for dead on the side of the road. Not only that, but just as the priest and the Levite avoided the hurting person and refused to offer help, we sometimes feel abandoned by the very people we thought we could rely on (Luke 10:25-37).

This has further caused a profound sense of loss and disorientation. It is as though a plague of darkness has descended, and we are desperately groping to find our way through the chaos (Exodus 10:22). We feel as though we are walking, and sometimes crawling, through the valley of the shadow of death, and the way is long, too long, and we are growing weary from it all (Psalm 23:4).

We ask of you today . . . with souls desperate for your intervention, that you hear our prayers and answer our cries (Psalm 102:1). Incline your ear to hear our pleas for mercy; we know we are not worthy; we know that no one living is righteous before you, and it is only by your grace we can now approach your throne (Psalm 143:1-2). With open hands we come to you, acknowledging our very lack. We cannot fix what is broken. We cannot heal what is ill. We cannot redeem what is captive. We cannot restore what is lost. But you can do all of this and more. You are the great Redeemer and Healer and Restorer. With compassion and steadfast love, be not far away from us now, Lord, for you are the only one who can help, you are the only one who can save (Psalm 22:11). Be gracious to us, Lord, and grant us your strength; show us a sign of your favor, for we are withering under the scorching heat of this suffering (Psalm 86:16-17). Guide us in the way we should go; help us to find refuge in you; teach us to do your will; and lead us on level ground (Psalm 143:8-10). Hold fast to us and never let us go, for we know we are completely reliant upon you.

We trust in you today . . . with every facet of our being, because you alone are able and faithful, so we cling to you in the dark, while waiting for the light of morning. For there is no one like you, and there is no one who can match your greatness (Psalm 86:8). For you are the great Wonder-Worker who whispers life into being. You are the God who speaks to dry bones and breathes new life into us (Ezekial 37:7-10). You are the God who removes our hearts of stone and replaces them with hearts of flesh. (Ezekial 36:26). So, we pray, right now, for [our loved ones] to know this same transforming power. We pray specifically for [our loved ones] to experience your grace and mercy and to have their hearts completely renewed by you. This is something only you can do. Only you, God, only you. Which is why we look to you, despite how dark and desolate our surroundings may be, because no one can save, but you.

We surrender to you today . . . with our whole hearts, Lord, we yield to you. We lay down our idols. We lay down our pride. We came into this world with nothing, and with nothing we will depart, which is why we lay everything at your feet (Job 1:21). All of our pain. All of our disappointments. All of our suffering. We give it all to you and ask that you redeem all of it. We know we come to you with nothing, yet you give us everything that is good. For that is who you are—you are the God who gives and the God who blesses. There is nothing good you withhold (Psalm 84:11), not even your only Son did you withhold (John 3:16). We know this to be true, even if our circumstances at this moment fail to seemingly show it; we know this world is not all there is; there is more to this life than we can see with our eyes; there is a world beyond this world, and we await with great hope the coming of your kingdom, when you undo all the sorrows of this world. This is why we pray for your kingdom to come, and your will to be done, on earth as it is in heaven. We live for that day, and until that morning dawns, we pray for your grace to sustain us and [our loved ones].

__We offer to you today__ . . . a sacrifice of thanksgiving in advance. For you have heard our pleas; you have accepted our prayers (Psalm 6:9). In our time of trouble, we have called on you and you have answered (Psalm 86:7). Because you, Lord, are merciful and gracious, abounding in love and faithfulness (Psalm 86:15). Your mercies are new every morning, and your compassion knows no end (Lamentations 3:23). So, we lift up our eyes to the hills, for we know from where our help comes; our help comes from you, the Maker of those very hills (Psalm 121:1-2). We thank you that you will not let our feet stumble, for you are our Keeper; you keep us, in our going out and coming in, you keep us from harm (Psalm 121:5-8).

__And we rest in you today__ . . . because of who you are. You are the God who invites the weary to come and experience your rest; you are the God who takes our burdens upon your shoulders and gives us a reprieve (Matthew 11:28-29). You are the God who exchanges our ashes for your beauty

(Isaiah 61:3). This is who you are. And while this may not yet be evident in our circumstances today, we trust it will be some day, either here or in eternity, because you know better than we do, how everything is held together in your nail-pierced hands. For even while you hung on the cross, you spoke the words that David once penned, of feeling forsaken (Psalm 22:1), and yet, you also knew that in three days' time the final words of that same psalm would also be true: That it shall be told "to the coming generation" of what you have done for "a people yet unborn" (Psalm 22:30-31). Because you knew, even then, even as total darkness covered the earth on that terrible Friday, that something good and beautiful was coming on Sunday. And now your scarred hands hold the promise that one day soon our current darkness will turn to light, too, all because of you. In the name of Jesus, we pray, your kingdom come, your will be done, on earth as it is in heaven. Amen.

CHAPTER 17

A Prayer of Petition

"Or which one of you, if his son asks him for bread, will give him a stone? . . . If you then, who are evil, know how to give good gifts to your children, how much more will your Father who is in heaven give good things to those who ask him!"

Matthew 7:9, 11

Ten syllables. That's how many syllables it takes to say the medical term for the type of blood clot I had in my brain. It's a kind that is exceedingly rare, but with a correct diagnosis and timely intervention, it's treatable. If it doesn't get diagnosed correctly and treated in time, the outcome is certain death. I almost missed the window. The doctors say I came within minutes of dying.

The more pressing question is: Why did a blood clot form in my brain in the first place? There are several medical possibilities, and after a slew of medical tests, an entire team of neurologists and hematologists said to me, "Denise, we just don't know what caused it." They looked for everything they could think of, and at the end of the day, they were stumped. All they could tell me is that I don't have any of the risk factors. I've gone for second and third opinions, and I've been told the same thing, "Denise, you're one of those rare anomalies we can't explain." Well, that's reassuring.

So, on the one hand, it's great that I've been given a clean bill of health. On the other hand, it's disconcerting that they cannot determine the cause of what nearly killed me. Does this mean it could happen again? At any point? Pretty much. I live each day with the blessing of a new day, knowing that on any given day, my body could form another clot, and I might not have a positive outcome the next time. This uncertainty, this unknowingness, is what I carry. But I know of so many who carry so much more.

I have a friend who has survived colon cancer. She rightly points out that breast cancer comes with a pretty pink ribbon, but there's no ribbon, she says, for butt cancer.[49] In my own way, I can relate. There's no ribbon for blood clots. Just ugly uncertainty. And with uncertainty comes the distinct feeling of *not* being in control. Which is never fun.

Then, on top of everything else, people like Job's friends will come along with their armchair-quarterback hypotheses; they'll offer advice and folk remedies, and they may even suggest that we're to blame for whatever ails us. But the Bible tells a different story. Life on this side of Genesis 3 means things don't always work the way they're supposed to. Bodies break. Systems fail. But God knows exactly what's happening inside our bodies and in the world around us. He has all the answers that all the smartest minds in the world cannot find. And it's in God alone we place our hope, for God is fully in control of every minute detail.

Now, we live each day in humble recognition that each new morning is a gift, and until our Bridegroom comes again and we experience that great wedding feast described in Revelation 19, we pray for our daily bread just as we pray for our other physical needs.

Gracious Father,

We look to you for our daily bread . . . *knowing that every good thing comes from your hand, for you are our Provider. When you formed us, you made us to require daily sustenance. This need is deliberate. It is meant to point us to you, our Sustainer. Which is why we ask for our daily bread, acknowledging our dependence on you. For you not only provide the beasts of the field with freshwater springs, and the birds of the air with branches for nests, and the livestock in the pasture with grass to satisfy, but you also provide for us, your people, with bread to strengthen our hearts (Psalm 104:10-15). Just as you provided new manna each morning for your people in the desert, you provide bread each day for us as well (Exodus 16:4-5). It all comes from you: first, in our ability to work, and second, in our opportunity to* *work. In the fulfillment of our duties, and in the recompense we receive, it all comes from you, so we thank you for the way you care for us, making sure we have what we need for life. Indeed, you are the source of all life. From the air in our lungs to the bread on our tables, it is all from you. And while there are times you call us to fasting, there are also times you call us to feasting. Both are from you. Because you are not a god who revels in our obvious lack, but you are the God who delights in filling our lack. For you are the Lord, our Shepherd, and in you we have what we need; you even prepare a table before us, and because of you, our cup overflows (Psalm 23:1, 5).*

We ask you today to show us the ways we can share our bread . . . *that you would help us to see the needs around us that we might be a blessing to others. Whether those needs are in food or other material things, help us to be your hands and feet, ministering to those around us, in our neighborhoods and our communities. But even as we look for ways to give much away, help us to see the times when we should also invite others in. Just as Abraham hurried to serve his three divine guests, promising a morsel of bread but delivering a feast instead, may we also feel a sense of urgency to invite guests to our tables (Genesis 18:1-8). For it is when we gather around the tables in our homes that we experience true fellowship of the soul. Breaking bread together in homes—it is what the early church did, with glad and generous hearts, and we want to follow in their steps.*

Just as they devoted themselves, to the teaching and the fellow-ship, and to the breaking of bread and the prayers, we want to do the same (Acts 2:42). And may we always remember that when we show hospitality to strangers, we may at times entertain angels unknowingly (Hebrews 13:2). Give us eyes to see the needs, Lord, that we might bring glory to your name.

We praise you, Lord, that you are the Bread of Life . . . *for as much as our frail bodies need daily sustenance, so also do our spirits need daily nourishment. And you, Lord, are the Bread from heaven, given to all who receive, that we might eat and be satisfied (John 6:35, 41). For you remind us that we cannot live on mere bread alone, but on every word that comes from you (Matthew 4:4). For the true bread is the Word of life, and we want to feast on your Word daily. Grow in us a healthy appetite to want more of your Word, filling us in ways that no earthly means can. May we taste and see that you, Lord, are good, and you fill us with good things (Psalm 34:8).*

We recognize, with the bread and the cup, the new covenant . . . *for the bread is your body, broken, and the cup is your blood, poured out. And the night before you died, you took the bread of the Passover and gave thanks, then you broke the bread and gave it away (Luke 22:19-20). Now, every time we gather with our brothers and sisters to worship you, Jesus, we remember your sacrifice on the cross. We remem-ber the price you paid. We remember how we could never* *make our way back into your holy presence, and that it is only through the torn veil, rent in two, the moment you exhaled your last, that access to your presence is now granted. So, we eat the bread, and we drink the cup, and every time we do, we proclaim the truth of you (1 Corinthians 11:26).*

We thank you for your provision, not only for bread, but also for all our physical needs . . . *for it is by your broken body that our brokenness is restored. It is by your wounds that we are healed (Isaiah 53:5). We understand that some healings happen in this lifetime, and others in the next, and while we cannot always understand why this is so, we know you are the only God who can restore, so in prayer we seek you today, both for ourselves and [our loved ones], for physical healing in our bodies. For you know us intimately, Lord; you saw us as we were formed in our mothers' wombs (Psalm 139:13). You know what we truly need, even more than we do, so we ask that you meet these needs, both the spiritual ones and the physical ones (Philippians 4:19). We know your ways are higher than our ways, for sometimes you merely say the word, as you did to the Roman centurion, and his servant, at that very moment, was healed (Isaiah 55:9; Matthew 8:5-13), and other times you use a certain means, as you did when you healed the blind man with mud! (John 9:1-12). Again, your ways are mysterious to us, but whether it is through your spoken word or your touch, or whether you choose to guide the hands that serve to heal here on earth, we ask for your healing power, both in our* *lives and in the lives of [our loved ones]. Like the woman who reached for the hem of your garment in faith (Mark 5:25-34), we are reaching for you today in faith. Like the woman bent in misery for years, we ask that you straighten whatever is bent in us and in [our loved ones] (Luke 13:10-17). Lord, we believe you are almighty; we believe you are all-capable; and we ask, that if there are any areas in our lives where unbelief lurks beneath the surface of our hearts, please help us in our unbelief (Mark 9:23-24). We pray that our tiny mustard seed of faith will grow, and that we will become persons of great faith by your gift of powerful grace (Matthew 17:20-21).*

Gracious Father . . . we pray that our tiny mustard seed of faith will grow, and that we will become persons of great faith by your gift of powerful grace.

We recognize that the bread you provide is nothing short of a miracle . . . *for you alone have the power to make something from nothing. For in a time of great famine, you sent Elijah to a widow, not in Israel, but in Zarephath, and you blessed her, with a jar of flour that refused to run empty and a jug of oil that never went dry, until the day you lifted the drought and brought rain upon the land (1 Kings 17:8-16; Luke 4:25-26). Here again, you are the God who orchestrates not only the weather but also the means of our provision. And when you taught the great crowds and healed the many who were sick, you had compassion on the* *hungry, for they were without means to satisfy their own pangs, so you took a small offering from a boy, of five barley loaves and two fish, and you gave thanks, then you miraculously multiplied the bread and the fish until all who ate were filled (John 6:1-15). Once again, you are the God of mercy who blesses assuredly and provides abundantly. So, we ask today that you do it again, Lord, do it again. When our cupboards are turning bare and we are struggling with finances, please provide us and [our loved ones] with the means we need. Help us not to eat the bread of idleness (Proverbs 31:27), but to step into your provision and work through the opportunities you have given. For we know that all good things come from you.*

We worship you as the Lord of all . . . *the Lord who answers our prayers for provision, and the Lord to whom all glory is due. We thank you that we can come to you, like the person in the story who knocked on his neighbor's door at night for bread, and the neighbor gave what was needed (Luke 11:5-8). That is who you are. You are the God who gives immeasurably more than anything we can think or dream or imagine (Ephesians 3:20). We thank you for the Bread of Presence that once sat in the tabernacle on the golden table; in two stacks of six, the twelve loaves represented your powerful presence and provision for your people (Exodus 25:30). And you are still present and providing for your people today (Matthew 28:20). For when* *you open your hand, we are filled with good things (Psalm 104:28). And our prayer today and every day is for your glory to go forth and endure forever, and for as long we live, that we may rejoice in your works and sing of your praise. In the name of Jesus, we pray, give us this day our daily bread. Amen.*

CHAPTER 18

A Prayer of Forgiveness

"Bear with each other and forgive one an-other if any of you has a grievance against someone. Forgive as the Lord forgave you."

Colossians 3:13 (NIV)

Almost immediately after I became an empty nester and committed myself to intercessory prayer, I experienced some deep wounds caused by others. Their actions were so hurtful that, for a time, it took me off my course. Instead of praying, I found myself perseverating on the wrongfulness of their actions. It couldn't have been a coincidence. The Bible is clear that unforgiveness hinders our prayers, so before I could move forward in prayer, I needed to forgive.

The psalms, again, are helpful. They express the reality of suffering—even suffering at the hands (and mouths) of others. The imprecatory psalms, of course, are discomfiting. They make us squirm. How can such vindictiveness be in the Bible when we're repeatedly told to love and forgive our enemies?

Psalm 109 is a prime example. It's a lament of how someone had wronged the psalmist with hurtful words, how someone repaid his friendship with evil (Psalm 109:1-5). But it's one thing to express lament, it's another thing to wish for that person's utter demise (Psalm 109:6-15). What are we to make of such passages in the Bible?

In a discussion on these curse-filled psalms, C.S. Lewis wrote:

> If the Jews [the writers of these imprecatory psalms] cursed more bitterly than the Pagans this was, I think, at least in part because they took right and wrong more seriously. For if we look at their railings we find they are usually angry not simply because these things have been done to them but because these things are manifestly wrong, are hateful to God as well as to the victim.[50]

The indignation we find in the psalms of cursing reflect a heart proclaiming that there is such a thing as right and wrong. They denounce any relativistic notion that "your truth" might be different from "my truth." They state firmly that some actions are just plain wrong. To this end, we can concur, but hopefully, we don't go so far as to wish harm on the wrongdoer. Here, as always, we look to Jesus as our example.

While on the cross and struggling to breathe, Jesus said, "Father, forgive them, for they do not know what they are doing" (Luke 23:34a, NIV). If anyone had a right to call down fire from heaven to consume his hateful murderous wrongdoers, Jesus—who being in very nature God—had that right. Yet, he "did not count equality with God a thing to be grasped, but emptied himself, by taking the form of a servant, being born in the likeness of men. . . . he humbled himself by becoming obedient to the point of death, even death on a cross" (Philippians 2:6-9). Jesus laid down his rights for vengeance and forgave instead, so now we follow Jesus's instruction in the model prayer to ask for forgiveness of our own sins and also to forgive those who have wronged us.

Gracious Father,

__We confess our sins to you today__ . . . for we know that we are just as much in need of your grace as anyone else, perhaps even more so. For anyone who claims to be without sin is deceived and inhabits no truth (1 John 1:8). For no one is righteous, not even one, for all have fallen short of your glory (Romans 3:10, 23). We confess that our hearts are prone to lead us down wrong paths—paths that lead toward self-reliance, self-trust, and self-justification. We want so much to believe

Gracious Father . . . when we turn our eyes on you, your Word shines a light on our feet, and in your great mercy, you show us the way home.

in our own sense of self-goodness, that our intentions are always pure and our motives always right. But your Word says otherwise (Jeremiah 17:9). Our hearts are tainted with self-interest, which shows itself when we preen with thinly veiled words and images that seek our own self-promotion. Oh, Father, forgive us. When our focus is on ourselves, we end up in the ditch of self-deception, hopelessly groping our way through the dark. But when we turn our eyes on you, your Word shines a light on our feet, and in your great mercy, you show us the way home. This is why you announced your earthly ministry with the simple words, "Repent, for the kingdom of heaven is at hand" (Matthew 4:17). For that is the door to freedom. Repentance. Which is why you invite us to ask, to seek, and to knock. For when we repent and ask for forgiveness, when we seek the light of your grace, and when we knock on the door to freedom, you have promised to answer us, to find us, and to open the door to us (Matthew 7:7). How great is your mercy, Lord!

We recognize that all sin required the cross . . . even our own. Forgive us, Lord, when we want to magnify the failings of others and minimize our own missteps. Forgive us, Lord, when we want to condemn the wrongness of others and justify the mishaps in us. For we know that our sin required the cross as much as anyone else's (James 2:10). For you became the propitiation of our sin by your blood, to become the justifier of those who put their faith in you (Romans 3:24-26). This is all a grace gift, granted by you and received by us. We did nothing to earn it or deserve it, lest we might boast in it (Ephesians 2:8-9). Just as you covered the nakedness of Adam and Eve with animal skins made from the shedding of blood, you have covered our shame by your shed blood on the cross (Genesis 3:21). You allowed yourself to be disrobed in shame, so that we might be robed in righteousness (Isaiah 61:10; Matthew 27:31; 2 Corinthians 5:21). May we never forget and never diminish what it cost you to forgive us and free us from our enslavement to sin. May we grow in humility, knowing we are sinners in much need of your grace.

We ask that you help us to grow in love . . . for you and for others. Because most of our sins, most of our shortcomings, most of our failures, are rooted in a lack of love for you and for others. Which is why your Word commands us to love our neighbors as ourselves (Leviticus 19:18). And there is no better example of how to do this than to watch how you lived your life while you walked this dusty earth. For you loved every human you encountered. You loved the broken and the hurting. You loved the lost and the wayward. You loved the deceived and the downtrodden. You even loved the ones who hated you and betrayed you, who mocked you and hurled insults at you. This kind of God-love is wholly other to us. It does not come naturally to us. But by your divine gift of grace, you can help us to love better and truer, you can show us how to love deeper and wider. This is what we ask today. That you grow our hearts in love.

We ask for the fruit of the Spirit of the living God . . . to take root in our lives and flourish to overflowing. In love and joy and peace. In patience and kindness and goodness. In faithfulness and gentleness and self-control (Galatians 5:22-23). May the fruit of repentance grow in our lives (Matthew 3:8), so that our neighbors and friends, and even our yet-to-be-friends, might see the difference in us—in eyes that gaze with warmth, in smiles that invite new friendship, and in arms that reach open wide. For when we love one another well, we bring honor to your holy name, for it is only by your transforming and redeeming love that we can love rightly, for you are love, and we can only love because you first loved us (1 John 4:7-8, 19).

We forgive those who have wronged us . . . because you have first forgiven us. And when we need to approach a brother or a sister who has sinned against us in some way, may we do so with great grace. May we follow your instructions and speak not to others about the offense; but may we go directly, with a heart desiring reconciliation (Matthew 18:15-17). May our words be true and our hearts be truer. May all we say and do be a reflection of you. May we become servants of mercy, for that is how you first treated us, for we know that we could never repay our own debts to you, so may we always be quick to extend that same debt-relieving grace to others (Matthew 18:23-35). For you declare in your Word that mercy triumphs over judgment (James 2:13).

We voluntarily choose to pay the price . . . of the wrongs done to us. And whenever a memory jolts us back to the pain of a former wrong done, help us to lay it at your feet, as many times as needed, and remind us again, that we have already forgiven in obedience to your Word, and help us to absorb the cost, again with more grace, because that is what you have done for us. Oh, let mercy rain down from heaven and wash our souls through. By your grace alone, we stand forever cleansed and right before you. Without spot or wrinkle, without blemish or stain (Ephesians 5:27). We glory in the goodness of you.

We seek your guidance as we walk each day in your grace . . . that we may be the kind of souls who are not easy to offend. Help us to be quick to overlook a slight. Help us to be swift to pierce darkness with light. May we bring to each moment a spirit of kindness, with a willingness to listen more and perhaps speak less. May we seek to understand and see more of the story that you are weaving throughout history. May we grow in wisdom and may this wisdom grow in humility. For we are forever humbly resting at your feet, looking to you, and learning from you. For you are our King. Today and always. In the name of Jesus, we pray, forgive us our debts as we also have forgiven our debtors. Amen.

CHAPTER 19

A Prayer of Protection

" . . . no weapon that is fashioned against you shall succeed . . ."

Isaiah 54:17a

The word *gospel* means good news, but I've heard some church people try to say that the gospel begins with bad news—with the fact that we're all sinners and we can't save ourselves.

While it's true we're born with a sin-bent nature and we need a Savior, the gospel doesn't begin with us. The gospel begins with a good God creating a good earth, and the people he made he called "very good" (Genesis 1:31). The original design was good, very good. But then, with a serpent and a lie and a human act of willful disobedience, it all went very bad (Genesis 3).

This is where we find ourselves today. Even at our births, we are born into the middle of an ongoing story, and we spend our lives learning how we fit into this overarching story of redemption that is unfolding under the heavens.

By God's grace, we are rescued from the spiritual death that accompanies life without God. Paul explained it this way:

> And you were dead in the trespasses and sins in which you once walked, following the course of this *world,* following the *prince of the power of the air,* the spirit that is now at work in the sons of disobedience—among whom we all once lived in the passions of our *flesh,* carrying out the desires of the body and the mind, and were by nature children of wrath, like the rest of mankind. (Ephesians 2:1-3, emphasis mine)

It's the old trifecta again—the world, the devil, and the flesh. These three primary forces work against all of us, but notice what Paul said next:

> But God . . . (Ephesians 2:4a)

But God being rich in mercy. But God being full of grace. But God being large in love. God did not leave us in a helpless state against such formidable foes. God left the glory of heaven and came to earth, cloaked in un-glory. He took on flesh and became like us in every way, except sinless. He paid our debt, giving his life in exchange for ours, setting us free from condemnation. Now, we have a new story to live out.

> For we are his workmanship, created in Christ Jesus for good works, which God prepared beforehand, that we should walk in them. (Ephesians 2:10)

God has good works planned for each of us to accomplish, and when we surrender our lives to Christ, we look to fulfill that which he has called each of us to do. But sometimes this good goal of serving God gets set on a bent path. For example, in another millennium, back when I was young and full of wide-eyed eagerness to serve God, I attended many youth conferences in the 1990s, where we were inspired to go and do great things for God! I think those conferences and conventions meant well, but too often we conflate greatness with worldly impressiveness.

When the values of the world seep into our ideas of what we think kingdom-living means here and now, we start to believe that doing great things for God means a big ministry or a big testimony or some other form of bigness. For most of us, though, genuine kingdom-living looks less like the last three years of Jesus's life and more like his first thirty years—ensconced in obscurity, walking dusty roads, and all the while knowing there's something more out there than the dailyness of life we experience right now. Because it's true, there is something more, but that more is still to come, when our Bridegroom returns.

In the meantime, the good works God has purposed for us to do might not look impressive in the world's eyes. It might look more like quiet living, devoting ourselves to our homes and our unglamorous workplaces. It might look more like humble serving, giving of our time and our resources in our local churches and communities. And it might look more like gracious loving, in our families and other relationships. In short, we live out the stories God has given us in the places where we already are. And we want to pray that nothing—not the world's values, not the evil one, not even our own fleshly desires—gets in the way of loving God and loving others. We don't want anything to pull us offtrack and prevent us from living out the story God has graciously placed us in, so we pray for God to lead us not into temptation and to deliver us from evil. We pray that our lives might be a testimony to the goodness of God.

The gospel is good news because it doesn't begin with us, and it doesn't center us in the story. We're in the story, but lo and behold, we're not the main character. Jesus is.

Gracious Father,

We pray for your help in understanding the Scriptures . . . *for you have told us that your Word is the Sword of the Spirit (Ephesians 6:17), and you have shown us that we fight against evil with the power of your Word (Matthew 4:1-11), and you have prepared us with the knowledge that this present age will bring tribulation (John 16:33), so we put on the whole armor of God—the belt of truth and the breastplate of righteousness and the shield of faith and the helmet of salvation—so that by your grace we may be able to withstand whatever comes our way (Ephesians 6:11-17). For at our births, we entered the story you are writing in our lives,* *as we live between the pages of Genesis 3 and Revelation 22, and we want our stories to bring glory to you.*

We pray for your grace to lead us away from temp-tation . . . *first from our own flesh, for we know that sometimes even good things can be turned into wrong things when they are taken to be ultimate things, for then they become idols in our hearts. Help us, Lord, to remain steadfast under such trials, for when we have withstood such tests, you have promised that we will receive the crown of life (James 1:12-15). We also pray for your grace to lead us away from the temp-tations we find in the world, for we know the values of the world are not of you and they do not line up with the truth of how you have designed this world to operate, and when we go against your good design for us, nothing but heart-ache and devastation will ensue.*

We pray for your mercy when we have sinned again . . . *for we do not want to stay in a place that does not honor you. May we be quick to seek forgiveness when we have fallen to temptation. Lord, strengthen us and help us to walk faithfully in your ways, for we cannot call you our King and then neglect the laws of your kingdom. For when your kingdom reigns in our hearts, our one desire will be obedience to your Word. Convict us, Lord, when we drift into apathy, or worse, cynicism. Forgive us, Lord, when we lose a sense of awe and wonder for how amazing you are. Lead us, Lord, to lift our eyes above our immediate surroundings and embed us deeply in your family. Grow us, Lord, firmer in the truth* *of your Word. Help us, Lord, to cultivate a deep contentment for everything you have already given us. Whether we have little or plenty, help us to be thankful in either circumstance (Philippians 4:11-12).*

***We pray for your protection and deliverance from things unseen . . .** for your Word tells us that spiritual forces are at work in ways our eyes cannot see. For you told us that Satan asked to sift Peter like wheat, so we know Peter struggled, not only with his own flesh and the world, but also with the powers of darkness against him (Luke 22:31-32), yet you also told us that you assured Peter you were praying for him, just as you are praying for us today (Hebrews 7:25). We also know from your Word that Satan was the unseen force afflicting Job in every way, but Job was not given this insight during his earthly life, yet still he served you (Job 1:6-11; 2:1-7). May we have the perseverance of Job and say with him that we know our Redeemer lives! (Job 19:25). In these stories and more, your Word shows us, again and again, that if you are for us, who can be against us? (Romans 8:31).*

***We praise you, Lord, that you are mightier than any power, seen or unseen . . .** and so we pray, Lord, that you deliver us and [our loved ones] from any attempts the forces of evil may try to take against us. With a shield of faith, Lord, we pray you deliver us and [our loved ones] from any flaming arrows that come our way (Ephesians 6:16). We thank you for the way you moved between the fleeing Israelites and* *the pursuing Egyptians, and you promised to fight on their behalf; they needed only to be silent (Exodus 14:14). Then you did it again on the cross, when you put yourself between us and death, and fought evil on our behalf. Now, by the blood of the Lamb and the word of our testimony, we can be overcomers (Revelation 12:11). And after we have suffered a little while, we pray that you will restore, confirm, strengthen, and establish us and [our loved ones] (1 Peter 5:10).*

We pray for your power to live our stories for your glory . . . *for we deeply desire to live this life you have given us in ways that are pleasing to you. May our prayers arise as incense before you (Psalm 141:2), and as you have blessed us, may we be a blessing to others. May we be known by our love, for we are covenant people. For you have entrusted to us the gospel, so we live and speak today, not to please others, but to please only you (1 Thessalonians 2:4). May we remain faithful to your Word and to our mission to the world. May we live our stories in such a way that others will know the Story of God is true. We thank you, Lord, that you hear our prayers, and you answer us when we call.*

Gracious Father . . . may we live our stories in such a way that others will know the Story of God is true.

We praise you, Lord, for you are the God who protects and delivers . . . *you are the God who saves and redeems. You are sovereign, and in complete control of everything.*

You even sing over us with your love (Zephaniah 3:17). In response, all we can do is praise you, for you, Jesus, are "the radiance of the glory of God," and you uphold the universe by the power of your Word, and now you sit "at the right hand of the Majesty on high" (Hebrews 1:3). So, we look toward that day when we will stand in your presence—in the throne room of heaven—when we will cast our crowns at your feet and sing with the angels, "Holy, holy, holy, is the Lord God Almighty" (Revelation 4:8). And we pray, in your holy name, Jesus, we pray, that with us there in your presence, [our loved ones] will stand alongside us too. Reach them, Lord Jesus. Soften their hearts and speak to them as only you can do. Just as you have entrusted the spreading of the gospel to us, we entrust the hearts of [our loved ones] to you. In all of this and more, we thank you and praise you. In your name, Jesus, we pray, lead us not into temptation, but deliver us from evil. Amen.

CHAPTER 20

A Prayer of Peace

"O, Lord, my Lord, the strength of my salvation; you covered my head in the day of battle."

Psalm 140:7

My home is filled with books. In almost every room, bookshelves line the walls, even in my closets. But in my bedroom closet, the bookshelves are stuffed with old journals because I've been writing out my prayers for years. First, I read God's Word, then at the top of the next blank page in my journal, I write out the passage of Scripture I most want to meditate on that day. Then I talk to God and write down my prayers. At the end of the year, I like to go back and reread my prayers from January through December. It's always amazing to see how God has answered so many of these prayers.

Rereading my prayer journals also reveals a distinct overarching storyline as it unfolds in my life and in the lives of those around me. It's impossible to miss how

God is truly the Author of our faith as he writes our stories (Hebrews 12:2). In his book *A Praying Life*, Paul Miller wrote:

> When life makes sense, it becomes a journey, a spiritual adventure. Writing down the adventure as it happens gives us a feel for our place in the story God is weaving in our lives. Journaling helps us to become aware of the journey.[51]

I know this to be true. Journaling—as a way of talking to God after reading his Word—helps us to become more aware of the providential storylines as they emerge in our lives. But what about those times when it feels like we've hit a dead-end and we can't figure out how we got there or how to get turned around and back on track? Again, Paul Miller explained, "Often when you think everything has gone wrong, it's just that you're in the middle of a story."[52]

That's how I felt when I woke up in the hospital after being in a coma for three days. I woke up in the middle of a new story that began to unfold while I was unconscious, and I needed to catch up with everything happening to me and around me. Jeff and I both felt like we'd been blind-sided by something we never saw coming. There were no warning signs. One morning everything seemed fine. The next morning everything was definitely not fine!

And remember when I said that my first thought after waking up was how God didn't answer my prayer? After being hospitalized four years earlier for pulmonary embolisms, I had prayed that God wouldn't allow blood clots ever to form in my body again. But there I was, in the hospital again, this time with a blood clot in my brain. This was not a story I wanted, and I felt like God had let me down in a pretty big way. At least, that's how I felt in that moment, and the evidence seemed to point in that direction.

Soon after I got home from the hospital, however, I pulled out my prayer journal. I wanted to go back and read what I had written before all this transpired. When I read the entries from days prior, I was stunned. I had been praying through the psalms, as is my custom, and when I had gotten to Psalm 86, I wrote down the following passage to mediate on it:

> Give ear, O LORD, to my prayer; listen to my plea
> for grace. In the day of my trouble I call upon you,
> for you answer me. (Psalm 86:6-7)

I wasn't in any trouble when I wrote those verses in my prayer journal. Life had been chugging along pretty well, but for some reason, those verses stood out to me that day. So, I wrote them down and made them my prayer. Then, just below those verses I wrote: *Psalm 88 is coming up in my reading. And I fear it echoes something else to come. I hope not. I pray not. . . . Lord, we need your grace to sustain us.*

I don't know why I sensed a Psalm 88 type of situation coming. (Remember, Psalm 88 is the psalm of darkness, the one without any hint of hope.) I've read and prayed through the psalms many times, and I had never felt that way before. But I prayed that day as the Spirit led me, and days later, I was suddenly and inexplicably near death. My husband said the doctors were grim in their interactions, so Jeff called our kids, two of them were away at college. He told them to come home right away, so they could say goodbye before I died.

I had wanted to devote my empty nest years to praying for my kids; instead, my adult kids surrounded my hospital bed and prayed for me while I laid there, unconscious and hooked up to a breathing machine. It was a Psalm 88 moment for our family.

But later, when I went back to read the prayers I wrote in my own handwriting, I realized God did answer my prayer! Not the one about never developing another blood clot, but the other one, the one asking for the Lord's grace to sustain us in a potential Psalm 88 moment.

God answered our prayers. He answered the prayer I had prayed earlier in my journal, and he answered the prayers my family prayed at the hospital.

I still have plenty of unanswered prayers in my journals. They're all sitting there on the bookshelves in my closet. You could call it my prayer closet. But I won't stop praying. I can't. God has proven himself faithful too many times.

Sure, there are moments when fear creeps in. What if I develop another blood clot? What will happen then?

Right after Jesus taught the model prayer, he then said, "Therefore I tell you, do not be anxious about your life. . . . which of you by being anxious can add a single hour to his span of life?" (Mathew 6:25-27). We live in a broken world where sometimes bad things happen. Sometimes it's a result of someone else's sin. Sometimes it's a result of our own sin. And sometimes it's just because the world isn't working the way it was originally designed to work. In this broken context, fear and anxiety may seem like reasonable responses, but no matter what may come our way, we can trust God is in control.

We have finished praying through each move in the model prayer, so I want to pray next about the thing that afflicts all of us to some degree—fear and anxiety. I don't mean to imply that if someone experiences anxiety that it's solely a "faith issue." I have loved ones who struggle with anxiety, and I understand that sometimes our bodies don't work right in this broken world. So, if anxiety is something you struggle with personally, the use of medication is something to talk with your doctor about, but even then, it's still good to pray.

Gracious Father,

We hear you, Lord, when you tell us not to fear . . . *for you say it, again and again, in your Word not to be afraid, and you often follow this command with the promise that you are with us, and then you promise further, to strengthen us and help us and uphold us (Isaiah 41:10). For you are our shield, you are our fortress, and in you, the Most High God, we take refuge (Psalm 91:1-2). This command—Fear not!—permeates your Word as a gracious reminder that, while there may be many things in this world that we could understandably be afraid of, we don't have to fear any of it because you are the Maker of this world, and you are sovereign over every living thing.*

We confess to you, Lord, that fear is something we sometimes contend with . . . *even though we know you are bigger than any fear we may face, yet there are still those moments when the worries of this life choke our joy and we experience fear—crouching, waiting, and ready to consume us. Help us, Lord, when fear looms close and threatens to overshadow us; help us to lift our eyes and fix our gaze on you, for when you are magnified in our vision, the veritable size of our problems recede, because the larger you are in our sight, the smaller our fears will be. We pray, Lord, that fear will have no place in our hearts and no foothold in our lives. We pray this for us and for [our loved ones]. We pray that your grace will replace any fears that linger still.*

We ask you, Lord, to replace our unrighteous fear with a righteous fear . . . for when we rightly learn to fear you and revere you as holy and mighty, then all those other fears fade. Again, in your Word you tell us that the fear of you is the beginning of wisdom (Proverbs 9:10). Help us, Lord, to understand better what it means to hold a right fear of you—a fear that reveres you as the one true God, holy and righteous and faithful. We want this kind of fear, the right kind, the kind that acknowledges how you are all-powerful and good. Lord, please exchange our unholy fears for a holy fear of you. Teach us, Lord, teach us and [our loved ones] that we may learn to live in the light of your righteousness for your name's sake.

We praise you, Lord, because you are the God of peace . . . for that is who you are. You are the Lord of peace, and true peace can come only from you (2 Thessalonians 3:16). For you declared in your Word that you give us your peace, and you do not give as the world gives, but you give wholly and freely (John 14:27). Even your name is called, "Wonderful Counselor, Mighty God, Everlasting Father, Prince of Peace" (Isaiah 9:6). So, we look to you today, our Prince of Peace. May your peace reign in our hearts and minds, and also in the hearts and minds of [our loved ones]. For your Word says that peace is a blessing from you (Psalm 29:11), so we pray for this blessing, for us and [our loved ones].

We invite you, Lord, into those situations where peace is sometimes hard to come by . . . *for as long as we inhabit this broken world, relationships will wobble under the strain of stress and anxiety, but you, Lord, are greater still. And you warned us ahead of time that trouble awaits us in this life, but you also promised us that you have already overcome whatever trouble this world may bring, and this is why we find peace in you alone (John 16:33). May we follow your command to "live peaceably with all," if at all possible, "so far as it depends" on us (Romans 12:18). For you tell us in your Word that it is to a person's honor to avoid strife, that only fools rush in to quarrel (Proverbs 20:3). So, we pray, Lord, that you grow kindness and patience in us, that we may love others well, with the same forbearing kindness and patience that you have shown us, for while we ourselves were still sinners, you gave your life for ours (Romans 5:8).*

We ask you, Lord, to help us to grow as true peacemakers . . . *for you promise us in your Word that peacemakers are blessed (Matthew 5:9). For this is what we desire, for our lives to be marked by your peace, that we may be known as peace-filled persons, devoted wholly to you. And whenever there is a conflict of any kind, may we seek your wisdom and guidance first, and may we become the light of Christ in our circumstances, bringing your peace with us wherever we go. May we be "eager to maintain the unity of the Spirit in the bond of peace," all for the glory of you, for you are "over all and through all and in all" (Ephesians 4:3, 6).*

We thank you, Lord, for the genuine peace you give us . . . *for your Word tells us that God-given peace is truly other-worldly, for your peace is something that surpasses our finite understanding (Philippians 4:6-7). And because of the peace you give, we can "lie down and sleep" (Psalm 4:8), trusting that you are holding all things together, while we rest. So, whenever life tumultuously thrashes all around us, like a storm-tossed boat at sea, may we be still in the midst of it all, because we know you are God, enthroned high above the heavens (Psalm 46:10). For you have shown us in your Word how to cultivate more of your peace in our lives, for peace is a fruit of the Holy Spirit (Galatians 5:22). You*

Gracious Father . . . we thank you for the genuine peace you give.

have promised in your Word that your peace will be with those who put into practice the instructions found in your Word (Philippians 4:9). So, we pray again for your Word to dwell in us richly, Lord (Colossians 3:16), and may our minds remain steadfast, keeping in perfect peace, because we trust in you (Isaiah 26:3). For the mind that is set on the Spirit is a mind that knows life and peace (Romans 8:6). For this we praise you and thank you. In your name, Jesus, the Prince of Peace, we pray. Amen.

CHAPTER 21

A Prayer of Thanksgiving

"She is clothed with strength and dignity;
she can laugh at the days to come."

Proverbs 31:25 (NIV)

Waking up from a coma is a surreal experience. In the following days and weeks, everyone around me celebrated. They had prayed for me, and now here I was, alive and well. For a while, I tried to join their happiness. But mostly, I needed a nap. And with each passing day, something quietly nettled me deep inside, like a dissonant chord refusing to resolve, until I realized I was on a different timeline from everyone around me.

When I first woke up, everyone else's experience was sheer relief. Their worst fears were over. Now they could rejoice. Which made sense. But for me, I didn't wake up *from* a nightmare, I woke up *to* a nightmare. Physically, I needed time to flush out all the drugs they had given me in the hospital, and I needed time for my body to heal—my voice had been badly damaged; it took months for my vocal cords to heal from being intubated. Emotionally, I needed time to process what had happened to me. Spiritually, I needed time to talk with God and come to a peace about all of it.

I needed time.

Then I remembered something an older woman told us two decades earlier when we were about to have a child. She said family members will sometimes begin celebrating the coming baby too soon. While the new mom is still laboring to give birth—and experiencing a curse-from-God level of pain—that's not the time to celebrate because that's disconnected from her current reality. But later, after the baby is born, and after the new mom has had a moment to catch her breath and recover, then it will be appropriate to celebrate the beauty of new life.

Her wise words helped me twenty years later to remember how people can experience the same event very differently, and in this case, my timeline hadn't yet synced up to everyone else's timeline. But after a few months—of praying, reading, journaling, healing, and taking long walks—I was finally ready to laugh again, and Jeff had a great idea. He booked a hotel for us in a beach town on the Atlantic Coast, where he also bought tickets for us to see our favorite Christian comedian live. He thought it might be fun to have an evening together where we simply laughed. I completely agreed, so we went away for the weekend and laughed.

Laughter really is the best medicine for the heart. (Proverbs 17:22)

Maybe for you, you're ready to laugh again after a long night of your own. Or maybe you're still so deep in the thick of sorrow that you can't imagine ever seeing the light of hope again. I want you to know it's okay to be where you are. It's okay to be on your own timeline for recovery. Our timelines will be unique to each of us. The good news is that the gospel promises our seasons of grief won't last forever. There's an expiration date on suffering. Our Bridegroom is coming.

There are days when I want Jesus to come back right now so all the heartache of this world will finally end. But then I think of the names still on my list, the ones I'm still praying for, the loved ones I desperately want to come to a saving faith in Jesus Christ. So, I ask God to help me wait a little longer, knowing that his timing will be right. And while we're waiting for that glorious day, we can pray.

If you've read my book *Deeper Waters*, then you know the last chapter of that book is titled "The Song We Sing." The book concludes on a note of thanksgiving. And in my book *Sanctuary*, the final chapter is a closer look at Psalm 150, the last song in the Psalter, which is a culminating song of thanksgiving. So, it's only fitting that the final prayer in this little book is a prayer of thanksgiving. It's a celebration of all that God has already done and all that he has promised to do.

Maybe you're ready to pray a celebratory prayer. Or maybe, if you're not quite ready to celebrate just yet (which

I totally understand!), you can make this an anticipatory prayer, depositing these words in your heart for the day when they will ring so true that you'll want to laugh with deep joy in response.

May the peace of God and the joy of the Lord reign in your hearts.

Shalom.

Gracious Father,

We thank you for the awesomeness of your Word . . . *from beginning to end, you have given us what we need to know who you are and why we are here. You have explained to us why the world operates as it does and how we need to live in order to thrive in this world you have created. May we live each day with thoughts and words and deeds that bring glory to your name. May we have hands that are eager to serve. May we have feet that carry the gospel to new places. May we have eyes to see the needs around us. May we have ears to hear the stories of how you are weaving all things together, to create a tapestry that we won't fully be able to see until we are with you in eternity. Until that day, we can know that, somehow, all things are working together to bring goodness to your kingdom here and glory to your name forevermore (Romans 8:28).*

We thank you for the way the psalms echo our day-to-day reality . . . for the one who arranged the order of each psalm did so with Spirit-inspired intention, for the lament songs are not lumped together in one heap, nor are the praise songs grouped together in a bunch; rather, the ebb and flow of the songs and themes resonate with reality. A psalm of praise will be followed by a psalm of lament, and so forth, just as we might experience a season of quiet followed by a season of grief, only to return to a new season of peace again at a later time. For this is how we experience life on this broken planet, riding the ups and downs of daily living, knowing that you are in control of every facet of our being.

We thank you for Psalm 88 . . . for the way your Word gives us permission to grieve while also welcoming us into your presence with our very real sorrows. Thank you for your abundant patience during our laments. Thank you, too, that your Word promises our mourning will one day be turned into dancing (Psalm 30:11). We thank you for the way Psalm 88 is followed by Psalm 89—another story-song of overarching praise, even in the midst of pain. For even though your people in that moment were experiencing exile, the psalmist knew that exile was not their permanent destination (Psalm 89:38-51). Restoration was coming, so Psalm 89 gives us a picture of real life, with bookends of praise, for it begins with festal proclamations of your faithfulness and steadfast love (Psalm 89:1) and it ends with a final once-and-for-all declaration saying, "Blessed be the LORD forever!"

(Psalm 89:52). This echoes our own lives, too, for when we became your child, the angels celebrated our salvation with joy (Luke 15:10), and one day soon, after this life of toil ceases, we will stand in your presence, and sing blessings to your holy name, and hear you say, "Well done, good and faithful servant" (Matthew 25:21).

We thank you for being a covenant-keeping God . . . for Psalm 89 again confirms that you are faithful to your Word (Psalm 89:3-5), for you promised David that his throne would never end (2 Samuel 7:1-17), and you accomplished just what you promised, when Jesus, born from the line of David (Matthew 1:1), lived a sinless life, then died and rose from the grave, and later ascended to the throne in heaven, where he now sits at your right hand (Hebrews 1:3). You are always faithful, Lord, to do what you said you would do, which is why we can place our whole trust in you, for you keep your promises, you stay true to your Word, and you fulfill your covenants. Even when we fail on our end, you never fail, for you are the same yesterday, today, and forever (Hebrews 13:8).

Gracious Father . . . you are always faithful to do what you said you would do, which is why we can place our whole trust in you.

We thank you for the whispers of the third day . . . for all throughout the Old Testament, from one generation to the next, you have shown yourself mighty, and your works have testified to your power, that you are sovereign over all things, and you are completely in control of every detail that unfolds. For you instructed your people to consecrate themselves, and you came down to Mount Sinai and you spoke to your people on the third day (Exodus 19:9-20). You led Abraham and Isaac on a three-day journey to Mount Moriah, to the very place where the temple would one day stand, and you spared Isaac's life, the only son of Abraham and Sarah, and you did it on the third day (Genesis 22:1-4). Scripture speaks of more third-day deliverances too. For on the third day, the cup-bearer was spared from execution and restored to his office (Genesis 40:1-13). When a decree in Persia threatened all the people of Israel, Esther called for a three-day fast, and on the third day she approached the king and you granted her favor, and as the plot unfolded, your people were spared (Esther 4:15-17; 5:1-2; 8:3-12). When Hezekiah fell ill and Isaiah said certain death awaited him, Hezekiah prayed for mercy and healing, and you heard his prayer and sent Isaiah back to tell him that on the third day he would go to the house of the Lord, and he would be restored (2 Kings 20:1-7). After three days and nights in the belly of a great fish, Jonah was safely delivered to land where he would preach repentance to the Ninevites (Jonah 1:17). Then in the New Testament, you did it again on the road to Damascus, where you spoke to Saul, the persecutor of believers, and you afflicted him with blindness; for three days he fasted and prayed in darkness, then you sent Ananias to heal him, and then you commissioned him to be a missionary, a preacher, and a writer (Acts 9:1-19). Lord, your Word is amazing. Only Someone outside of time could have threaded together this third-day theme across multiple millennia—all to foreshadow the greatness of your might and your mercy. How great and awesome you are!

We thank you that on the greatest Third Day you rose from the grave . . . *for this is of "first importance," that you "died for our sins in accordance with the Scriptures," that you were buried but then raised to life again on the Third Day (1 Corinthians 15:3-4). For no power is greater than the power of the Lord our God, for on the Third Day you defeated death and proclaimed victory over evil. Now we live, set free from sin, for you purchased our freedom with your blood. And none of this was a surprise to you, for you knew before the beginning of time what you would do. You told the disciples, and all who would hear, that you would suffer and then rise again in three days (Matthew 12:40; Mark 8:31). Then you did what you said you would do. Just as you always do. You keep your Word. So, we praise you and thank you because you are a covenant-keeping God! And we thank you that you are coming again, to make all things new—a new heaven and a new earth—where you will erase all sorrow and wipe every eye dry, where there will be no more pain and no more death, and where all the darkness and sadness of today will become former things that will have passed away (Revelation 21:1-4). And until that day comes, we will pray.*

We will pray . . . *for your name to be hallowed and for your kingdom to come. We will pray for our daily bread and for the forgiveness of our sin. We will pray for your help as we forgive others, and we will pray for your protection. We will pray for [our loved ones], that you will meet them on their own road to Damascus, that you will open the eyes of their hearts (Ephesians 1:18), that you will redeem them from the clutches of the enemy, and that you will set their feet on a firm foundation, that they may stand among the witnesses who bear testimony to your name. And all the while, we will pray that our lives are a reflection of you, and that you will receive all the glory for the wonderful, transforming, redeeming love that you bestow on us, by your sweet lavish grace. We thank you, Lord, that you hear our prayers. What a gracious God you are. In the name of Jesus, we pray, forever and always. Amen.*

AFTERWORD

"Shadrach, Meshach, and Abednego replied to the king, 'Nebuchadnezzar, we don't need to give you an answer to this question. If the God we serve exists, then he can rescue us from the furnace of blazing fire, and he can rescue us from the power of you, the king. But even if he does not rescue us, we want you as king to know that we will not serve your gods or worship the gold statue you set up.'"

Daniel 3:16-18 (CSB)

Several years ago, a friend of mine suddenly and unexpectedly passed away. With no warning, her heart stopped beating. She was only in her thirties, and she left behind a husband and four sweet daughters. The news of her death hit me hard. *Why would God take her? Why would God allow this to happen to her girls?*

Over the next few days, I scrolled through social media on my phone and read the tributes that our mutual friends posted about her. Each tribute offered kind words with fond remembrances. In like manner, I tried to muster together the words I wanted to say, but the lump in my throat wouldn't go away.

Then it happened. I read a particularly beautiful tribute to our friend on social media. Then, the very next day, that same person posted again, this time asking for a recommendation for a new dishwasher. Or maybe it was a washing machine. It was a household appliance of some kind, and it left me slack-jawed.

One day we're mourning the loss of a beautiful person; the next day we're crowdsourcing for a new dishwasher.

This is what social media does. It collapses time and distance. The events that are seriously life-altering for some people become little more than a tidbit of news for others, a mere blip on the radar for far-flung people who are not much affected.

That was the day I began to distance myself from the cultural milieu online. Social media is not where genuine friendships are found. The real thing is found in real time and space, in an embodied community, with people with whom you can share a meal and have a face-to-face conversation.

The more I distanced myself from the worldly expectations found in online spaces, the more I embraced the people around me—my neighbors and my church family. And the more I invested in local relationships, the more I felt called to pray for the individuals I know personally. Rather than fill my mind with newsy updates about people far and wide, I sensed a calling to pray for the people God had already placed in my everyday life. I eventually deleted (not just deactivated) all of my social media accounts.[53] I wanted to devote my time and my focus to more worthy endeavors.

But as soon as I began to pray, with an intentional focus on intercession, I experienced inordinate setbacks.

In the space of four years, I had two near-death experiences. That sounds awfully strange to write. Believe me, it's even stranger to experience. But it's true. Inexplicably true. And it's left me with a gnawing question: *Why did I live while my young friend passed away?*

Time Is Short

We want so much to believe that all we must do is exercise and eat right, and then, with healthy habits in place, we can ensure long life. We want so much to believe that we can control our destiny with the right choices. But sometimes we can be completely healthy and then out of nowhere get hit with something entirely unforeseen and unexplainable.

I don't know why I lived and my friend didn't. There are some questions we'll never know the answers to until we're on the other side of eternity, but I do know this: Time is short. Shorter than we even realize. Our lives are but a "mist that appears for a little while and then vanishes" (James 4:14). A mist. A vapor. And then . . . gone. And I don't want to waste a single minute on worthless things.

How we spend our days is how we spend our lives.

Some people have suggested that I write more about my near-death experiences because people want to know if I went to heaven for a few minutes or something dramatic like that.

Those stories sell.

But as I've said before, I've developed an allergy to drama.[54] It's not my thing. What is my thing? Telling the story of Grace.

Telling the story of how the Bible has become a lifeline and a tether to all that is good and beautiful and true.

Telling the story of how hope is possible in the darkest of moments because real Hope is a person, and his name is Jesus.

Telling the story of why prayer is the breath of my being, and I live to pray for those around me.

This is my story. This is my song.

Time is short, so I'm choosing to spend my days with the people nearest me, where I live and work and worship. And more than ever, I'm choosing to spend my time praying for those I love—including those I'm trying to love.

Even If

As I write this, I'm waiting for the results of a recent biopsy. Not for me, but for one of my adult children. Right now, my family is in a state of limbo. Waiting. We don't know what the results will be. Obviously, we're praying and hoping for a report of "no cancer present."

It's in moments like these we most urgently get on our knees.

Once again, I'm interceding for a dear loved one, not knowing what the outcome will be. And yet, everything I've studied and learned and practiced and shared about prayer is still true.

Even if the biopsy results are not what we pray and hope they'll be, God is still God. And prayer is still his invitation to come to him with both our hurts and our hopes. Prayer is a divine promise that God will be with us no matter what comes our way.

Perhaps it's a coincidence, or maybe just ironic, that I've devoted the past two years to learning more about prayer. I've read dozens of books on the subject. I've studied The Lord's Prayer in Scripture, and I've read multiple commentaries on the Gospels of Matthew and Luke, where this model prayer is found. To better understand the wider context of The Lord's Prayer, I opened my home and invited women to come over on Saturday mornings to study the Sermon on the Mount. I also spent a year meeting with women in my community to study the Gospel of Matthew. To further immerse myself in biblical prayer, I wrote out every psalm in longhand. And every step of the way, I prayed. I prayed in secret, alone in my home, and I prayed with others, in biblical community, because prayer is never meant to be a dissected thing, studied in an academic or abstract manner. Prayer is the blood and guts of humanity crying out to God.

By the time this little book on prayer reaches your hands, the results of my child's biopsy will be known. We'll either be thanking God for allowing this particular dark cloud to pass over us at this time, or we'll be trudging through the next steps of surgery or chemotherapy or both. Either way, God will still be God, and prayer will still be the way we reach out to him in earnestness. But one thing I won't be doing is sharing the results of this biopsy in any public manner. The story surrounding this biopsy belongs to my adult child, and they can share their own story in their own way when they are ready.

In the meantime, I'll keep wearing my mom hat—praying on the sidelines and in waiting rooms—sometimes on my knees with head bowed, begging God for mercy, and sometimes on my feet with hands raised, shouting praises to heaven.

I'll also keep inviting my friends to join me in prayer, together, while waiting for morning.

A QUIET INVITATION

*"On the Sabbath day we went outside the city
gate by the river, where we expected to find a
place of prayer. We sat down and spoke to the
women gathered there. A God-fearing woman
named Lydia, a dealer in purple cloth from the
city of Thyatira, was listening. The L*ORD *opened
her heart to respond to what Paul was saying."*

Acts 16:13-14 (CSB)

The story of Lydia in the Bible is one of my favorites.

While Paul and the other disciples traveled around Asia
Minor proclaiming the gospel, Europe, at this point, was
still unreached (Acts 16:6). Then God told Paul in a dream
to chart a new course for Macedonia, which is modern-day
Greece (Acts 16:9-10).

Upon his arrival, Paul discovered this region didn't have
a synagogue, which meant few if any Jews inhabited the
area. But he heard about a group of women who gathered by
the river to pray on the Sabbath. Paul went to the river and
preached the gospel to the women, and Lydia was among
them. She responded to the gospel immediately, and the first
church in Europe was born.[55]

Today, we can be like Lydia and invite our friends to
join us in prayer.

An Invitation to Pray

My hope for this little book on prayer is that it might serve as a quiet invitation for people to pray. This little book is not meant to be an exhaustive encyclopedia regarding every topic pertaining to prayer, but it may, hopefully, serve as a catalyst to ignite a passion for prayer in the hearts of those who are yearning for a deeper life in Christ.

To this end, I want to continue what has begun in these pages. I do not wish to stop writing about prayer and move on to another topic; rather, I intend to continue with deeper discussions and more prayers, especially with regards to the Psalms.

Eugene Peterson once wrote:

> I knew that following Jesus could never develop into a 'long obedience' without a deepening life of prayer and that the Psalms had always been the primary means by which Christians learned to pray everything they lived, and live everything they prayed over the long haul.[56]

The Psalms guide us through our human experiences, giving us the words we can pray, so I want to invite you to join me online, where I'll be writing in more depth on the psalms and sharing more prayers. You can find me here: denisejhughes.com. And like Lydia, you can invite a friend to join you, and together we can dive deeper into the heart of God through prayer.

Shalom.

NOTES

1. Hamilton, Ian. "3 Things You Should Know about Psalms." Ligonier Ministries, July 12, 2023. https://learn.ligonier.org/articles/3-things-psalms.

2. Wiersbe, Warren. *Be Worshipful: Glorifying God for Who He Is—OT Commentary on Psalms 1-89*. David C. Cook. 2004. p.276.

3. Linneman, Jeremy. *Pour Out Your Heart: Discovering Joy, Strength, and Intimacy with God through* Prayer. B&H Publishing. 2025. p.43.

4. Whitney, Donald. *Praying the Bible*. Crossway. 2015. p.37.

5. Elsesser, Kim. "CNN's Don Lemon Says Nikki Haley Is Past Her 'prime' at 51-Here's What Research Says." Forbes. June 3, 2024. https://forbes.com/sites/kimelsesser/2023/02/16/cnns-don-lemon-says-nikki-haley-is-past-her-prime-at-51-heres-what-research-says/. Accessed April 10, 2025.

6. Wiersbe, Warren. *Be Delivered: Finding Freedom by Following God—OT Commentary on Exodus*. David C. Cook. 1998. p.196.

7. Merida, Tony. *Christ-Centered Exposition: Exalting Jesus in Exodus*. Holman Reference. 2014. p.198.

8. Bonhoeffer, Dietrich, *Life Together*. Harper One. 1954. p.58.

9. Murray, Andrew. *With Christ in the School of Prayer*. Aneko Press. 1885, 2018. p.16.

10. Hughes, Denise J. *Deeper Waters*. Harvest House Publishers. 2017. p.98.

11. Pink, Arthur W., *The Beatitudes and the Lord's Prayer*. Baker Books. 1979. p.80.

12. Linneman, Jeremy. *Pour Out Your Heart: Discovering Joy, Strength, and Intimacy with God through* Prayer. B&H Publishing. 2025. p.85.

13. "Agnus Dei." Performed by Michael W. Smith. Accessed May 7, 2025. *https://youtube.com/watch?v=alJOStsdw3s*.

14. Bernstein, Elizabeth. "The Case for Being Ungrateful." Wall Street Journal. Nov. 24, 2024. Accessed April 13, 2025. https://wsj.com/lifestyle/relationships/gratitude-industry-mental-health-thankfulness-5030cc92.

15. Ibid.

16. Vroegop, Mark. *Dark Clouds, Deep Mercy: Discovering the Grace of Lament*. Crossway. 2019. p.29.

17. Hughes, Denise J. "Grief, Gratitude, and a Gentle God." April 12, 2024. https://denisejhughes.substack.com/p/grief-gratitude-and-a-gentle-god.

18. Akin, Daniel. *Christ-Centered Exposition: Exalting Jesus in the Sermon on the Mount*. Holman Reference. 2019. p.94.

19. Pink, Arthur. *The Beatitudes and the Lord's Prayer*. Baker Books. 1979. p.101.

20. Ibid. p.101.

21. Murray, Andrew. *With Christ in the School of Prayer*. Aneko Press. 1885, 2018. p.20.

22. Pink, Arthur. *The Beatitudes and the Lord's Prayer*. Baker Books. 1979. p.108.

23. Akin, Daniel. *Christ-Centered Exposition: Exalting Jesus in the Sermon on the Mount*. Holman Reference. 2019. p.97.

24. Ibid. p.96.

25. Akin, Daniel. *Christ-Centered Exposition: Exalting Jesus in the Sermon on the Mount*. Holman Reference. 2019. p.98.

26. Tripp, Paul David. *Quest for More*. New Growth Press. 2007. p.159.

27. Wiersbe, Warren. *Be Loyal: Following the King of Kings—NT Commentary on Matthew*. David C. Cook. 1980. p.58.

28. Alsup, Wendy. *I Forgive You: Finding Peace and Moving Forward When Life Really Hurts*. The Good Book Company. 2022. p.82.

29. Keller, Timothy. *Forgive: Why Should I and How Can I?*. Viking. 2022. p.167.

30. Lewis, C.S. *Reflections on the Psalms*. Harper One. 1958, 1986. p.28-29.

31. Alsup, Wendy. *I Forgive You: Finding Peace and Moving Forward When Life Really Hurts*. The Good Book Company. 2022. p.10.

32. Keller, Timothy. *Forgive: Why Should I and How Can I?*. Viking. 2022. p.170.

33. Pink, Arthur. *The Beatitudes and the Lord's Prayer*. Baker Books. 1979. p.116.

34. Akin, Daniel. *Christ-Centered Exposition: Exalting Jesus in the Sermon on the Mount*. Holman Reference. 2019. p.100.

35. Lewis, C.S. *The Screwtape Letters*. Harper One. 1959, 2009. p.3.

36. Whitney, Donald. *Spiritual Disciplines for the Christian Life*. NavPress. 1991, 2014. p.200-213.

37. Murray, Andrew. *With Christ in the School of Prayer*. Aneko Press. 1885, 2018. p.80-81.

38.   Ibid. p.81.

39.   Linneman, Jeremy. *Pour Out Your Heart: Discovering Joy, Strength, and Intimacy with God through* Prayer. B&H Publishing. 2025. p.152-153.

40.   Peterson, Eugene. *A Long Obedience in the Same Direction: Discipleship in an Instant Society.* InterVarsity Press. 1980, 2000. p.145.

41.   Whitney, Donald. *Praying the Bible.* Crossway. 2015. p.11.

42.   Wiersbe, Warren. *Be Loyal: Following the King of Kings—NT Commentary on Matthew.* David C. Cook. 1980. p.57.

43.   Card, Michael. *A Sacred Sorrow: Reaching Out to God in the Lost Language of Lament.* NavPress. 2014. p.23.

44.   Ibid. p.25.

45.   Hughes, Denise J. "How I Left the Prosperity Gospel." September 18, 2023. https://denisejhughes.substack.com/p/how-i-left-the-prosperity-gospel.

46.   Peck, Scott. *The Road Less Traveled: A New Psychology of Love, Traditional Values and Spiritual Growth.* Touchstone. 2012. p.50.

47.   Brueggemann, Walter. *The Message of the Psalms: A Theological Commentary.* Augsburg Publishing House. 1984. p.53.

48.   Ibid. p.52.

49.   Hardy, Niki. *One-Minute Prayers for Women with Cancer.* Harvest House Publishers. 2022.

50.   Lewis, C.S. *Reflections on the Psalms.* Harper One. 1958, 1986. p.35.

51.   Miller, Paul E. *A Praying Life: Connecting with God in a Distracting World.* NavPress. 2009, 2017. p.258.

52.   Ibid. p.207.

53.   Hughes, Denise J. "7 Reasons Why I Finally Quit Social Media." March 4, 2024. https://denisejhughes.substack.com/p/7-reasons-why-i-finally-quit-social.

54.   Hughes, Denise J. "I Have Developed an Allery to Drama." November 17, 2023. https://denisejhughes.substack.com/p/i-have-developed-an-allergy-to-drama.

55.   Hughes, Denise J. *Word Writers: Philippians.* Harvest House Publishers. 2016. p.13-14.

56.   Peterson, Eugene. *A Long Obedience in the Same Direction: Discipleship in an Instant Society.* InterVarsity Press. 1980, 2000. p.6.

No part of this book—nor anything I have ever published—has been made with Artificial Intelligence (AI) or ghostwriters. All of my words, including any accidental typos, are my own, except for when I quote others with appropriate citations.

ABOUT THE AUTHOR

Denise J. Hughes is a teacher at heart. She loves to connect with women through inspiring stories and biblically based messages. With an M.A. in English, she's taught college composition and literature, and she's the author of several books. She spends her days investing in her local community, serving women through a community Bible study. From her quiet nest in North Carolina, Denise enjoys long walks with her husband, where they savor the changing colors of the trees.

Connect with Denise

denisejhughes.com

denisejhughes.substack.com

ALSO AVAILABLE

FROM

DENISE J. HUGHES

Deeper Waters

Deeper Waters explores the many ways the ancient text of the Bible connects with our lives today. You don't have to be a graduate student in seminary to be a serious student of the Bible. Through genuine stories, Denise shows you how to hear God's voice through the pages of his Word and discover a joy you never thought possible when reading the Bible.

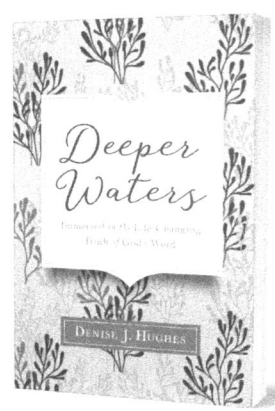

Sanctuary

Sanctuary invites you to step away from the clamorous noise in the world all around you and find refuge in the quiet truths of God's Word. Through this 31-day devotional, you will learn how to cultivate the "quiet life" that Paul speaks of in 1 Thessalonians 4:11-12. With a heart centered on Christ, it really is possible to live each day with a clear focus, a quiet confidence, and a steady peace.

www.ingramcontent.com/pod-product-compliance
Lightning Source LLC
Chambersburg PA
CBHW051619120626
46551CB00014B/1865